Hengistbury Head

Archaeological Sites

General Editor: Malcolm Todd
Reader in Roman Archaeology,
University of Nottingham

Hengistbury Head

Barry Cunliffe

Professor of European Archaeology
University of Oxford

Paul Elek London

First published in Great Britain in 1978 by
Elek Books Ltd
54–58 Caledonian Road, London N1 9RN

ISBN 0 236 40125 4 (cased)
ISBN 0 236 40107 6 (paperback)

Printed in Great Britain by
The Camelot Press Ltd, Southampton

Contents

Figures

Preface

For 10,000 years Hengistbury Head has been actively used by man. Initially, Palaeolothic and Mesolithic hunting groups roamed and camped over the hill; later, from the third to first millennium, communities of farmers lived and buried their dead here; and finally, in a brief and brilliant episode, a group of traders occupied the site, and, protected behind massive defensive works, engaged in long-distance commerce with the Mediterranean and the Atlantic seaboard. The evolution of Hengistbury as a port of trade is crucial to our understanding of the social and economic development of Britain in the period 100 B.C.–A.D. 50—a period which saw the end of the old order and the establishment of a settled urban economy. It was a time of dramatic change, when cross-channel contacts were rapidly developed only to be dislocated by the campaigns of Caesar; when the vital trading systems which had suddenly come into being in a time of freedom were manipulated and deflected by the growing power of Rome. Hengistbury lay in the forefront of these events: it is a site unique in British history and as such deserves the attention which I hope this book will focus on it.

What I have here attempted is simply to summarize the evidence available to us at present, and to examine this evidence against an historical and an economic framework. Inevitably more questions are posed than are answered, but herein lies the fascination of the subject. If this book does little more than to renew interest in Hengistbury and to emphasize its remarkable potential, it will have served its purpose.

In preparing this work I have received much help from many friends and colleagues. In particular I would like to thank John Lavender of the Red House Museum, Christchurch, for his many kindnesses. He has generously put much unpublished material at my disposal and has read the first draft of this book, offering much helpful comment and criticism. His infectious enthusiasm has been a great encouragement. Many other museum directors and assistants have helped by correspondence and by making collections available to me. Among them John Renouf (Jersey Museum), Rona Cole (Guernsey Museum), Mansel Spratling (British Museum) have taken much time in showing me material in their care and answering questions about it. But this work could not have been contemplated without the ready cooperation of Sir George Meyrick, who has allowed me to examine and to draw important material in his collection at Hinton Admiral. I have also received much help and advice on the Hengistbury coins from Melinda Mays and Colin Haselgrove, to whom I gratefully offer my thanks.

Finally, I would like to record my debt to my colleagues at the Institute of Archaeology in Oxford for their assistance in so many ways. Mike Rouillard was responsible for producing all the drawings which illustrate this volume, Bob Wilkins and Nick Pollard prepared most of the half-tone illustrations, Tim Ambrose critically read the text and offered many helpful comments, while Angela Ambrose, with great patience, produced the typescript. To my friends and colleagues who have made this work possible I extend my grateful thanks.

Barry Cunliffe
Oxford
June 1977

1
The site and its early exploitation

Hengistbury Head is a peninsula 1·5 km long which juts out into the sea from the east coast of Dorset. Along its southern side it is scoured constantly by the winds and waves, but to the north lie the more tranquil waters of Christchurch Harbour, into which flow the two great Wessex rivers, the Stour and the Avon. Geologically the Head is composed largely of the Tertiary Bracklesham Beds—in this area a deposit of sand overlying loamy clay—which here contain large concretions of ironstone. In the nineteenth century this ironstone was of commercial value and was collected or dredged from the shore and quarried in quantity from the north face of Warren Hill, where the quarry scars and waste tips of this early industrial landscape can still be clearly seen (fig. 3). The Bracklesham Beds, exposed in the southern cliff face, rise to a height of 15 m, above which there is a capping of river gravel, thought to be part of the first Lower Taplow Terrace (Green 1946), adding a further 2 m in height.

The south side of the Head is under a constant battering from the sea. Bushe-Fox (1915, 6) records that 10–12 m was eroded from the cliff in the vicinity of the Iron Age earthworks between 1907 and 1912, and a comparison of the Ordnance Survey maps of 1915 and 1962 shows that a further 25 m has been washed away. No doubt the removal of ironstone boulders from the beach during the period of quarrying in the nineteenth century would have allowed the sea to be more destructive, but even before that there is evidence of extensive erosion. The sketch map published by Grose in 1779 (fig. 17) shows the Iron Age earthworks curving inwards on the south side. A rough estimate would therefore suggest that in the last 200 years 150 m of land has crumbled away into the sea. In recent years this danger has been alleviated to some degree by the construction of a breakwater, to control longshore drift and create a wide protective beach, but still erosion continues.

On the north side of the Head the situation is quite different. The two rivers, the Stour and the Avon, carry a considerable load of alluvium to the sea, part of which is deposited in the harbour. The current and the tides tend to keep the main channels free, but in the lee of the Head, and protected by the single bar which the sea has built out from it, an extensive area of marshland has formed (fig. 2).

One further process has contributed to the Hengistbury landscape—the wind-assisted movement of loose sand derived largely from the beach and

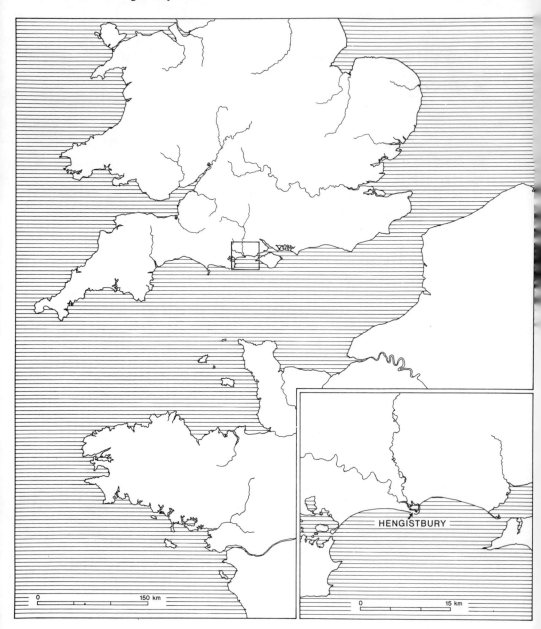

Fig. 1 The location of Hengistbury.

Fig. 2 *opposite* Hengistbury from the air looking northwards across Christchurch harbour towards Christchurch. The Iron Age earthworks known as the 'double dykes' can be seen bottom left, Warren Hill is bottom right. (Photograph: Dr J. K. St Joseph: Committee for Aerial Photography, University of Cambridge)

carried inland by the off-sea convection wind. The blown-sand layer varies in thickness: in many areas it is absent, but behind the main Iron Age rampart it reaches a thickness of 2 m. The sand will continue to shift in the wind for as long as the vegetation cover is broken, as it now is by the continual tramping of visitors and holiday-makers.

These, then, are the processes now at work sculpting the Head, but in the more distant past the situation would have been decidedly different. Throughout the greater part of the Quaternary era Hengistbury would have been far inland on the north side of the hypothetical 'Solent River', which at this time is thought to have flowed west–east through the bottom of the syncline of the Hampshire basin, bounded on the south by an upturned rim of chalk forming a continuous range of hills linking the chalk ridge of Purbeck with that of the Isle of Wight. Throughout the Ice Age the river and its tributaries, like the ancestors of the Stour and Avon, would have been constantly regraded as the sea level rose and fell. The gravel deposit on the

Head was probably laid down beside the Stour and Avon during an interglacial episode when the sea level was high and the lower stretches of the Solent river would have been a wide estuary. During the last glaciation the river appears to have been graded to 25–30 m below present sea level, resulting in a deep down-cutting of its tributaries which caused the breaching of the southern chalk ridge. In early postglacial times the rapid rise in sea level (the Flandrian transgression) caused by the melting ice, led to the flooding of the Solent river valley and in consequence the widening of the gap through the chalk barrier. Gradually the remnants of the chalk were destroyed by sea action, leaving only the Needles as a reminder of the last stages of its disintegration. Once the barrier was gone, the winds and tides could drive against the soft tertiary rocks of the now-exposed Hampshire coastline, relentlessly scouring away the friable cliffs to form the two great bays of Poole and Christchurch. Hengistbury Head, still subject to these pressures, is but the remaining extremity of the ridge which once divided the upper reaches of the Solent River from its Stour/Avon tributary. In the last 12,000 years or so the sea must have advanced some 4 or 5 km.

Hengistbury Head would always have provided an attractive environment to man. With the sea not far distant to the south and with the wide river valleys immediately to the north, sea birds, fish and other forms of wildlife would have abounded. It is hardly surprising that camp sites of Upper Palaeolithic and Mesolithic hunters have been found. The same resources would have continued to attract men throughout the rest of the prehistoric period. Large collections of Neolithic and Bronze Age flint implements scattered over the headland reflect use, and probably sporadic settlement, throughout the third and second millennia. Towards the middle of the second millennium, barrows containing cremation burials began to be constructed, thirteen of which still survive as prominent landmarks. The next evidence for human use is provided by the remains of a small Iron Age settlement dating to the sixth–fifth century B.C., one of the many which clustered along the fertile fringes of the Stour and Avon valleys. Thereafter the picture is unclear until some time about 100 B.C. when Hengistbury suddenly emerged as a major port, having developed close contacts with overseas traders, particularly those coming from Normandy and Brittany. It was probably at this time that the earthworks, built across the neck of the promontory to protect it, took on their final form.

This brief period of intense activity, lasting not much more than a hundred years or so, is Hengistbury's most significant phase, for at this time Hengistbury can fairly be claimed to have supported the first truly urban community in Britain. While settlement of some kind certainly continued throughout the rest of the Iron Age and much of the Roman period, it does not appear to have been on the same highly organized level as it had been in the early first century B.C.

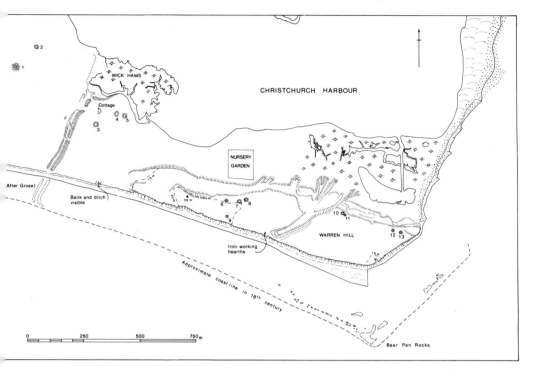

Fig. 3 General plan of Hengistbury showing approximate position of the coast line in the eighteenth century.

At the end of the Roman period the site was abandoned and so it has since remained. In the early twelfth century it is mentioned as *Hednesburia* in a grant of land made to the Canons of Christchurch. By the seventeenth century it is referred to as *Hynesbury*, a name which takes on its present spelling, Hengistbury, only in the nineteenth century, in the period of antiquarian romanticism when many prehistoric earthworks were assigned, without good reason, to well-known historical personalities.

The birth of archaeological interest

The development of Bournemouth, from a tiny village of less than 700 souls in 1851 to its present size, approaching a population of 200,000, has inevitably disturbed and destroyed many square miles of a landscape which has proved to be unusually rich in archaeological finds. Fortunately there lived in Christchurch an antiquarian, Herbert Druitt, whose fame as a collector was well known to the local labourers employed in working the gravel pits and digging house foundations. Between 1906 and 1940 he amassed an enormous collection of archaeological material, which, together with its supporting documentation, was eventually transferred to the Red House Museum at Christchurch.

The first significant finds to be made on Hengistbury consisted of a collection of Iron Age and Roman pottery, found on the north side of the Head in 1909. This was supplemented early in the next year by a small group of Celtic coins. Thus, when in July 1910, the owner, Sir George Meyrick, offered the entire headland for sale, it was clear to Druitt that a valuable archaeological site was likely to be threatened by further urban expansion. After an unsuccessful appeal to the National Trust to intervene, he persuaded the Society of Antiquaries to take the initiative and to mount what was essentially a rescue excavation.

The direction of the work was entrusted to J. P. Bushe-Fox. 'I was authorized to start operations in December, 1911,' he writes, 'fully believing that a few weeks' work would be all that was necessary, but so much was found that the excavations had to be continued for over six months. In that time an area of over forty-two acres was explored and three large barrows were dug out' (Bushe-Fox 1915, 1).

His excavations of the settlement site began just east of the double dyke and continued along the shore of Christchurch Harbour in the lee of Warren Hill. His method was to dig long narrow trial trenches and to extend laterally when something of interest was encountered, a style of digging which had the advantage of sampling large areas while at the same time destroying a minimum amount of archaeological evidence (fig. 4). His published report, which appeared three years after the excavation had ended, presented his findings in a degree of detail unusual for the time. In addition to describing the barrows, he listed and discussed 58 separate features relating largely to the Iron Age occupation. This was followed by an extensively illustrated record of the finds, including chemical analyses of a group of metallurgical samples. In short, the report was a thorough and scholarly piece of work of outstanding value.

The excavation awakened interest in the site, and by the end of 1912 a plan to build eighty houses was dropped. There followed an abortive scheme for the construction of a golf course, but after some preparation of the low-lying areas in 1912, involving extensive ploughing, the syndicate collapsed (Calkin 1966, 8). A few years later the site was bought by H. Gordon Selfridge who intended to build a large mansion for himself on the headland, but this project too was eventually abandoned and all that remains of the scheme is the Nursery Garden, now the Bird Observation and Ringing Station.

Selfridge was sufficiently interested in the archaeology of the site to employ H. St George Gray as archaeological consultant. Work was due to begin in the summer of 1918, but the economic state of the country, in the latter

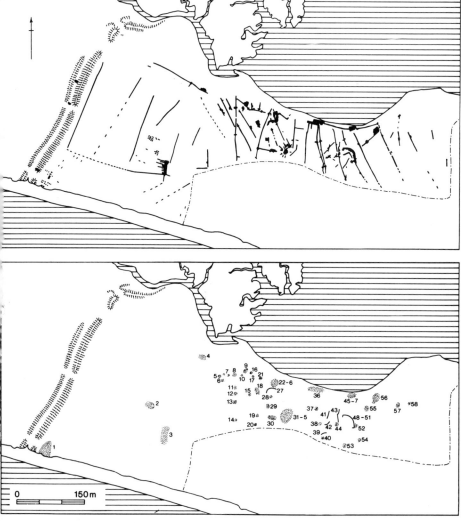

Fig. 4 The excavations of Bushe-Fox, 1911–12. The upper plan shows the positions of the excavation trenches, the lower plan indicates the location and extent of the individual 'sites'.

months of the Great War, was serious. In a letter to Druitt dated 3 July 1918, Gray wrote, 'after reading the debate in the House of Commons, on the Labour and Harvest question, in yesterday's papers, excavation at the present time seems almost impossible'.

Work eventually began after the harvest in September 1918 in the area of the Nursery Garden, which was then being laid out, and continued to the following April. Attention then turned to the examination of seven of the barrows, which was to take from April to November 1919. The results were unspectacular. In the autumn of 1919 it was decided to trench the area to the west of the Nursery Garden in an attempt to pick up more of the Iron Age settlement which Bushe-Fox had discovered—a programme which was to continue sporadically until 1924, during which time a further barrow was excavated. The result of the seven-year campaign was that a quantity of Bronze Age, Iron Age and Roman material had been recovered, but little significant advance in knowledge had been made. The excavations were never published but the notes, drawings, photographs and finds are now preserved in the Red House Museum at Christchurch.

The last serious threat to the site finally passed when in 1930 the Bournemouth Corporation bought the entire headland in order to preserve it as a public open space and recreation area.

In more recent years there have been three archaeological excavations, all of limited extent. The first, in 1957, consisted of a series of trial trenches sited at the south-western extremity of the Head. The work, directed by Angela Mace, was concerned to examine an area where a scatter of Upper Palaeolithic flints had been found by Druitt after the ploughing of 1913, and later confirmed by Calkin in a number of trial pits dug in the 1950s. The excavation of 1957 resulted in the full publication of an Upper Palaeolithic site of considerable significance (Mace 1959). The site was further examined by Dr John Campbell in 1968 and 1969, when erosion of the cliff edge threatened to destroy the rest of the stratified remains. The third post-war excavation was undertaken by Dr David Peacock in 1970, and consisted of several trenches dug on the shore of Christchurch Harbour where erosion was destroying the archaeological levels. Here a series of well-stratified occupation layers of the Iron Age and Roman period were recovered.

Apart from this work, constant observation by John Lavender of the Red House Museum, Christchurch, has led to the noting of a number of significant archaeological details, and casual finds continue to be made.

Upper Palaeolithic settlement

The earliest evidence of man at Hengistbury was discovered high on Warren Hill at the south-easternmost extremity of the peninsula. Here, after the ploughing of 1913 and at the instigation of Herbert Druitt, many thousands of flint implements were collected. Although most of the material was of

Fig. 5 *opposite* Upper Palaeolithic flint implements. Scale 2/3.
1 Burin (after Mace 1959, fig. 5, no. 28).
2 Burin (after Mace 1959, fig. 5, no. 20).
3 Shouldered point (after Mace 1959, fig. 9, no. 76).
4 Backed blade (after Mace 1959, fig. 9, no. 4).
5 Scraper (after Mace 1959, fig. 9, no. 50).
6 Shouldered point (after Mace 1959, fig. 9, no. 19).

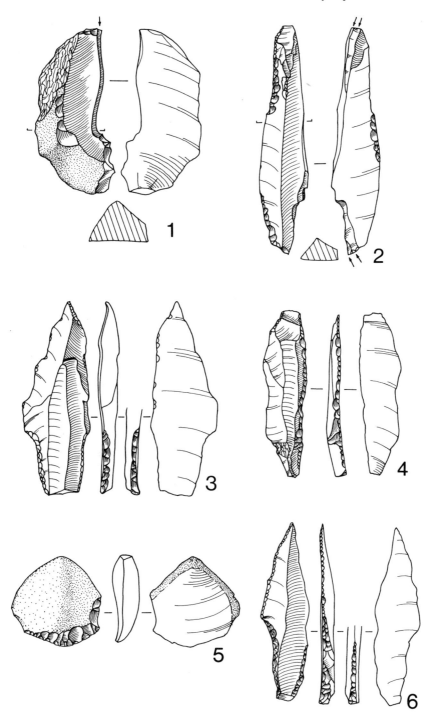

Neolithic and Bronze Age date, one group could be distinguished from the rest: it included tanged points, a shouldered point and several large backed blades, all closely similar to material of Upper Palaeolithic date found distributed extensively over north-western Europe. Sites of this date are extremely rare in Britain. In all only some 25 are known, and of these 21 are caves. Hengistbury is thus one of the very few open sites of Upper Palaeolithic date known in Britain.

Trial trenches carried out in 1967 soon established that much of the area had been extensively disturbed by ploughing, but an unploughed strip some 17 m wide survived along the cliff edge. Here an area of about 80 square metres was totally excavated (Mace 1958). Flint implements and waste material were found at all levels in the sand from 23 to 70 cm. In all probability they had been dropped on to the soft sand over a comparatively limited period of time and had been trodden into the surface.

In all, over 2,200 flints were found in 1957, of which about eleven per cent could be classed as tools, including tanged points, backed blades, burins, scrapers, awls, and saws, representing the complete lithic element in the tool kit of an Upper Palaeolithic hunting group (fig. 5). The importance of the find and the fact that erosion was constantly eating into the cliff face at this point led to another excavation in 1968–9 in which a further 4,400 flints were recovered.

It was impossible to date the occupation by absolute methods, e.g. radiocarbon or pollen dating, but the Hengistbury assemblage clearly belongs to the Creswellian industry, which elsewhere, on cave sites, has been dated by radiocarbon assessments to between 12,000 and 8,000 B.C. The presence of tanged points, however, appears to distinguish the Hengistbury assemblage from those found in the British caves, but suggests that it can be compared more closely with continental sites, in particular the Ahrensburgian industry of north Germany and the Netherlands, and the material from Bromme in Denmark (although it must be admitted that in neither case is comparison exact). In terms of the pollen zonation, which is used to describe the climatic and vegetational changes over the whole of north-west Europe, the Bromme and Ahrensburgian industries can be shown to belong to zones II and III (the Allerød and the Younger Dryas periods), which are securely dated to the bracket 10,000–8,000 B.C. Thus it was in this period that Upper Palaeolithic hunting groups probably camped on Hengistbury Head.

Mesolithic occupation

Evidence of Mesolithic occupation is less secure, but a few flint implements of Mesolithic type were recorded in the humus layer sealing the Upper Palaeolithic site, and others have been collected from time to time from various locations on the promontory. Such a favourable environment is hardly likely to have been overlooked by hunting and gathering groups of this period.

Neolithic–Early Bronze Age occupation

The fourth to the second millennia was a period of activity at Hengistbury, to judge by the considerable number of flint implements recovered by surface collecting and from excavation. No occupation traces have, however, yet been found *in situ*, nor have the many hundreds of implements been catalogued or studied. All that can safely be said is that the collection includes scrapers, knives and arrowheads typical of the Neolithic and Early Bronze Age.

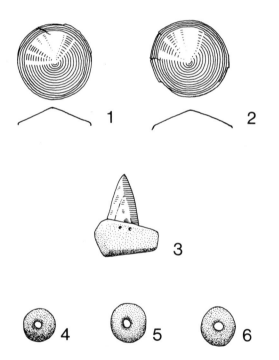

Fig. 6 Small objects from barrow 3. Scale 1/1.
1, 2 Gold coverings to conical shaped buttons (B.-F. M. Col.).
3   Halberd pendant of amber and copper alloy (B.-F. M. Col.).
4–6 Amber beads (B.-F. M. Col.).

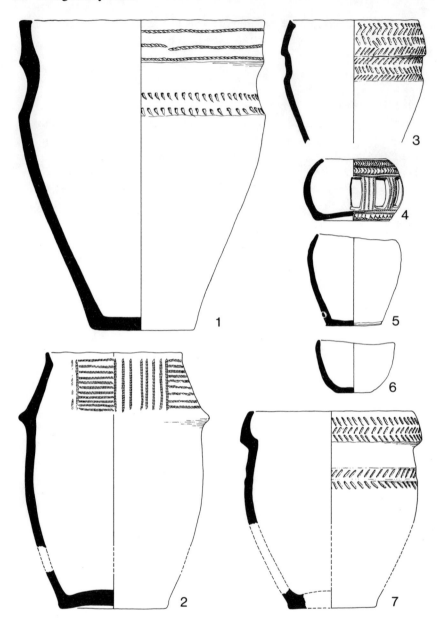

The Bronze Age cemetery

In the early part of the Bronze Age, Hengistbury was used as a cemetery, represented now by the thirteen barrows which still survive in recognizable form. Two lie to the west of the Iron Age defences, three immediately to the east, the remainder are sited on Warren Hill. All have been indicated and numbered on fig. 3. Three (nos. 3, 6 and 7) were examined by Bushe-Fox in 1911–12, while the rest of those which lie within the defences were excavated by St George Gray, nos. 4, 5 and 9 to 13 in 1919 and no. 8 in 1922. That other burials, unmarked by barrows, may possibly remain to be found, is suggested by the discovery of a flat bronze axe of Early Bronze Age date close to barrow 10 on Warren Hill (fig. 9, no. 1). Although no trace of a burial was found at the time, and the axe may have been accidentally lost, it is at least a possibility that it once accompanied an interment. Whether or not many unmarked graves remain, it is clear from the surviving evidence that in the early second millennium Hengistbury was occupied by an extensive cremation cemetery. Brief descriptions of the barrows and their burials are given below in Appendix B (pp. 83–5).

The Hengistbury burials consistently date to the first half of the second millennium B.C. Barrow 3 is particularly informative, since its contents are typical of the rich graves of the so-called 'Wessex Culture' of the Early Bronze Age, and all of the objects can be closely paralleled among the Wiltshire 'Wessex burials' (fig. 6). The closest in content to Hengistbury is Wilsford grave 8 which contains, among other things, a slotted incense cup, a halberd pendant and a gold-covered conical 'button'. Upton Lovell, Wilts., produced similar gold-covered buttons, as well as amber beads, while Preshute grave 1 was provided with a halberd pendant (for comparative material see Piggott 1938, and Annable and Simpson 1964). The collared urn from barrow 3 (fig. 7, no. 1) is also of a type commonly found in Wessex graves, and has been

Fig. 7 *opposite* Bronze Age pottery from the barrows. Scale 1/4.
1 From barrow 3.
   Reddish-brown fabric with coarse grits (B.-F. M. Col.).
2 From barrow 6.
   Soft black fabric with occasional quartz grits (B.-F. M. Col.).
3 From barrow 12.
   Soft black ware (SGG. Red House Mus.).
4 From barrow 3.
   Smooth light-grey ware (B.-F. M. Col.).
5 From close to barrow 1.
   Brown ware with sparse flint and shell gritting (1935. Red House Mus.).
6 From close to barrow 1.
   Smooth brown fabric with sparse angular flint gritting (1935. Red House Mus.).
7 From barrow 4.
   Soft reddish-brown fabric (1958. Red House Mus.).

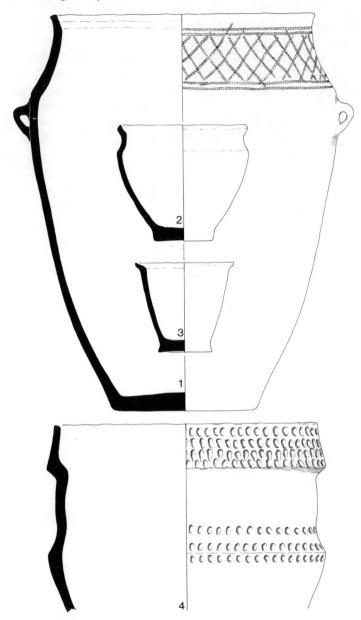

Fig. 8 Bronze Age pottery from barrow 7 (all B.-F. M. Col.). Scale 1/5.
1 Light-brown ware with white grits.
2 Coarse black sandy ware.
3 Coarse black ware with some sand tempering.
4 Coarse black ware with occasional grits.

tentatively assigned by Longworth to his 'Early Series' of urns (Longworth 1961, 289), which originated from native Neolithic tradition and was eventually superseded some time about 1600 B.C. or a little before. Thus the cremation burial in barrow 3 can be regarded as an outlying representative of a series of aristocratic graves belonging to the Early Bronze Age and dating to some time in the first half of the second millennium.

The other burials are less clearly datable, but the elegant biconical urn from barrow 7 (fig. 8, no. 1) with its strap handles and cord decorated neck, belongs to a series of vessels named after the Cornish site of Trevisker (ApSimon and Greenfield 1972). Trevisker series pottery was densely distributed in Cornwall and Devon, but was transported further east in smaller quantities into Wiltshire, Dorset and Hampshire, the Hengistbury vessel being one of the easternmost finds (ibid., fig. 1). Precise dating is not possible, but the vessel is likely to have been made some time between 1700 and 1500 and is therefore broadly contemporary with the Wessex style burial in barrow 3. All the other vessels from the Hengistbury cemetery are likely to fit within this time bracket. The cemetery therefore appears to have been in use for a comparatively short period of time.

One further point which both Bushe-Fox and St George Gray noted was that all the barrows examined contained quantities of flint flakes and some flint implements scattered within their mounds. These presumably originated from the earlier occupation of the immediate neighbourhood. The implication would seem to be, therefore, that the cemetery developed only after the Head had been opened up by settlers, and, indeed, it may be that burials were deliberately sited on land which had become of marginal value through over-use.

The Christchurch area was densely occupied in the third and second millennia, as the evidence recorded on fig. 10 will readily demonstrate. Cemeteries of barrows and urnfields straggle along the ridges, from Hengistbury westwards and from Christchurch north to St Catherine's Hill, while on the terraces above the flood plains spreads of artifacts indicate areas of occupation. Evidently the population was dense (Calkin 1969), and the land was extensively utilized at least by the end of the second millennium.

Hengistbury Head may have been abandoned for several hundred years between the time that the Early Bronze Age cemetery went out of use, in the middle of the second millennium B.C., and the appearance of settled occupation which began in the early Iron Age in the sixth or fifth century B.C. During this time, however, occupation in the neighbourhood appears to have been intense, as the nine urnfields and several large scatters of finds of domestic character imply.

The earliest Iron Age settlements: 700–400 B.C.

Within the area defined by fig. 11, ten separate areas of occupation assignable to the beginning of the Iron Age have been recognized, of which two lie on Hengistbury Head.

The pottery of this early phase, broadly 700–400 B.C., is distinctive. The commonest type is the large jar, usually fairly coarsely made, with an upstanding or outbent rim. The finer wares include small bowls, often coated with haematite, a red oxide of iron, and heavily burnished to create a shiny

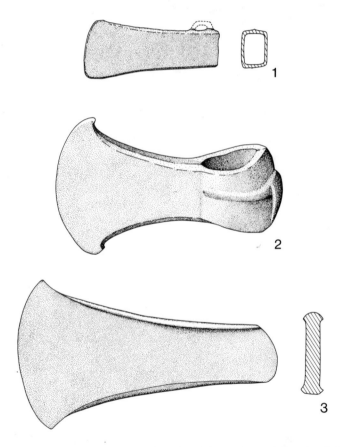

Fig. 9 Bronze Age implements from Hengistbury and its neighbourhood. Scale 1/2.
1 Breton palstave from Hengistbury (B.-F. Brit. Mus.).
2 Sicilian shaft-hole axe from Southbourne (chance find. After BM, Guide to *Later Prehistoric Antiquities* fig. 8, no. 2).
3 Early Bronze Age axe from close to barrow 10 (chance find 1953 Red House Mus.).

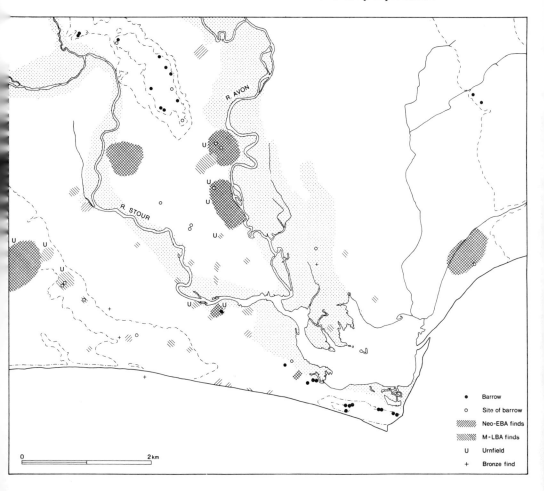

Fig. 10 Distribution of Neolithic and Bronze Age settlements in the Hengistbury region. Stipple shows extent of alluvial deposits.

finish. As might be expected, during this period of 300 years or so, pottery styles changed significantly. In the early stage the coarse vessels were usually heavily impressed with fingertip and fingernail decoration on the shoulder and rim, and were sometimes accompanied by large jars with decoration incised in geometric patterns, inset with white paste. The bowls of this phase were often of bipartite shape with rims beaded and shoulder angles emphasized with cordons. The zone between the shoulder and lip was sometimes decorated with incised or stamped decoration. Another type, often found at this time, was the tripartite jar with sharp shoulder and outflared rim. Assemblages of

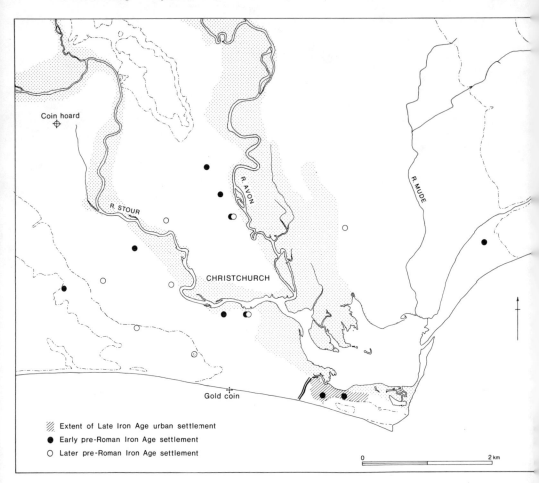

Fig. 11 Distribution of Iron Age settlements in the Hengistbury region. Stipple shows extent of alluvial deposits.

this kind are widespread in southern Britain and have been referred to as the Kimmeridge–Caburn style after two sites where the types are well represented (Cunliffe 1974, 33–4). In the Hengistbury area no large or well-defined groups of the early phase have been identified, but vessels showing the general characteristics of the style are known from Hillbrow and from Hengistbury itself (fig. 12, nos. 6–9, 14, 15, 17).

In the later phase the coarse wares tended to become less heavily impressed with fingertip decoration while the bowl types, now regularly haematite coated, developed flared rims and were frequently decorated with horizontal rilling on the shoulders. These general characteristics, with regional variations, can be paralleled on many sites in Wessex and neighbouring areas. Typically, they are referred to as the Late All Cannings Cross–Meon Hill style but distinctive Somerset and Dorset varieties can be defined (Cunliffe 1974, 37–8). Vessels of this style are common at Hengistbury and stylistic links with central Wessex are close (fig. 12, nos. 1–5, 10–13).

Bushe-Fox recognized this group of early Iron Age pottery as something quite distinctive and, at the time, very little known elsewhere. He grouped all the early types together and referred to them as class A (Bushe-Fox 1915, pls. IX and XVI). Class A pottery was found at at least six separate locations on the promontory (sites 2, 3, 30, 31, 33 and 44) but it was only at sites 30 and 3 that these early types were discovered in sufficient quantity and relatively free from later material to suggest undisturbed areas of early occupation. Elsewhere, class A material was sparse and the sherds were usually mixed with much larger quantities of later pottery.

Site 3 covered an area of some 400 square metres within which six hearths of clay and stones were recorded. Apart from pottery the only other finds were a zoomorphic bronze (fig. 30, no. 6) and several hundred flint flakes which may have been of earlier date. Site 30 was smaller, covering some 88 square metres. No structures were recorded, but again quantities of flint flakes were noted. The two sites are sufficiently far apart to suggest that they may represent two separate settlement locations. Their chronological relationship is difficult to distinguish, but site 3 produced more pottery of the earlier Kimmeridge–Caburn style than did site 30. If this is significant then it could be that site 30 succeeded the settlement on site 3.

Of the status of the settlements there is little that can be said. In all probability they represent the farms of single family units typical of those settlements which occur elsewhere in the area and are found extensively in neighbouring parts of Wessex. It remains a possibility, however, that the earliest phase of the double dykes or of the now obscured earthwork, may belong to this period (below p. 35). If so, then Hengistbury could be regarded as an early hillfort.

Two isolated finds deserve to be mentioned here. On site 33, where some early (class A) pottery was found, Bushe-Fox discovered a socketed bronze axe of Breton type (fig. 9, no. 1, and Bushe-Fox 1915, pl. XXX, 12). Axes of this kind were widely distributed on both sides of the Channel in the seventh and sixth centuries, and reflect widespread trading contacts between Brittany and southern Britain. It is possible that these axes, which were often unused and even unfinished, were ingots of bronze—a convenient form in which to transport the metal (Briard 1965, 241–82; Giot 1960, 156–61). The other object is altogether more unusual—a bronze shaft-hole axe of Sicilian type (fig. 9, no. 2) found in the sea about 3 km west of Hengistbury where it had

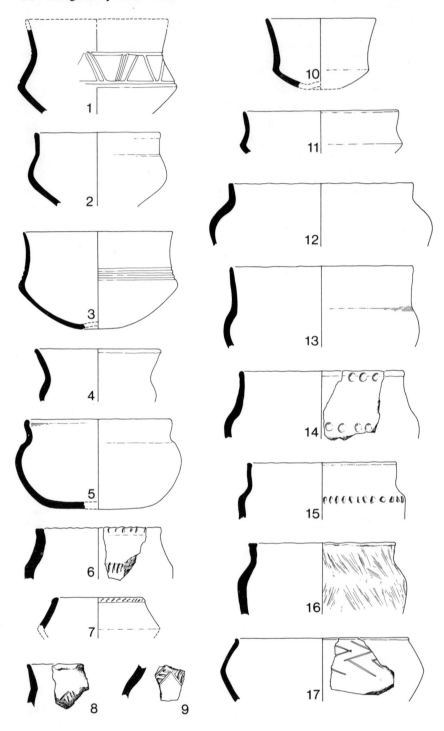

either been lost overboard from a boat or had eroded out of the cliff. The axe is probably eighth century in date and, if a genuine ancient loss, it can be claimed to reflect the widely flung trading contacts which are known to have been in operation along the Atlantic seaways at this time. The two bronzes together hint at the potential significance of the Hengistbury peninsula as a convenient landfall for long-distance trading expeditions.

The middle phase of Iron Age occupation: 400–100 B.C.

There is very little archaeological material from Hengistbury which can, with certainty, be assigned to this period, largely because no well-stratified groups have been recorded, but a number of individual pottery types can be selected from the collection to compare with material of this date found in stratified contexts on neighbouring Wessex sites.

Hengistbury lies close to the boundary between two differing ceramic traditions—a Dorset tradition called the Maiden Castle–Marnhull style, and the 'saucepan pot' styles which were widely distributed in Hampshire and Wiltshire. As might be expected, pottery of both styles is represented at Hengistbury.

In fig. 13 a selection of vessels of the Maiden Castle–Marnhull style is presented, all of which represent types which can be found in Dorset in third- and second-century B.C. contexts. These types, however, also continue in use

Fig. 12 *opposite* Early Iron Age pottery. Scale 1/4.

1   Smooth grey ware with some grits. External haematite coating (B.-F. Brit. Mus.).
2   Smooth grey ware with grog tempering. External haematite coating (B.-F. Brit. Mus.).
3   Hard black sandy ware. External haematite coating (B.-F. M. Col.).
4   Reddish-brown sandy ware. External haematite coating (B-F. Brit. Mus.).
5   Hard grey sandy ware, roughly burnished (1977 Private Col.).
6   Sandy ware fired red (B.-F. Brit. Mus.).
7   Dark grey-brown sandy ware (B.-F. Brit. Mus.).
8, 9   Fine grey sandy ware with sparse flint grits; burnished surface, probably same pot (B.-F. Brit. Mus.).
10   Smooth black ware fired brownish-black (B.-F. Brit. Mus.).
11   Grey sandy ware with burnished haematite coated surface (B.-F. Brit. Mus.).
12   Hard grey sandy ware. External haematite coating (B.-F. Brit. Mus.).
13   Black sandy ware with flint grits. External haematite coating (B.-F. Brit. Mus.).
14   Grey-brown ware with flint grits (B.-F. Brit. Mus.).
15   Smooth grey ware with some flint grits (B.-F. Brit. Mus.).
16   Coarse grey sandy ware, roughly wiped (B.-F. Brit. Mus.).
17   Grey sandy ware with sparse flint grit tempering. Black burnished surface (B.-F. Brit. Mus.).

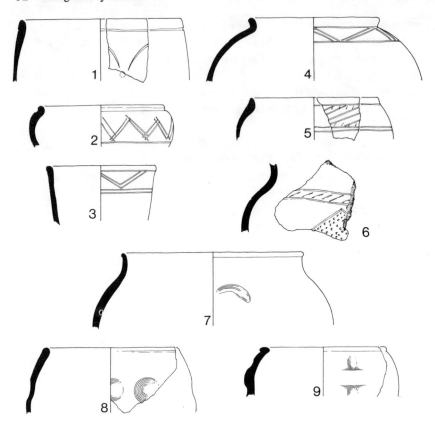

Fig. 13 Middle Iron Age pottery. Scale 1/4.
1 Hard grey sandy ware, burnished surface (B.-F. Brit. Mus.).
2 Smooth grey ware with flint grits; burnished surface (B.-F. Brit. Mus.).
3 Black sandy ware with flint grits; burnished surface (SGG. Red House Mus.).
4 Grey-brown ware with flint grits; burnished surface (B.-F. Brit. Mus.).
5 Hard grey sandy ware; burnished surface (B.-F. Brit. Mus.).
6 Smooth grey ware with flint grits; burnished surface (SGG. Red House Mus.).
7 Hard grey sandy ware (B.-F. Brit. Mus.).
8 Grey sandy ware (after Bushe-Fox 1915, pl. XXVIII, 42).
9 Light-brown sandy ware (after Bushe-Fox 1915, pl. XXVIII, 44).

into the first century B.C. and therefore cannot be used to prove an occupation
before *c.* 100 B.C. Similarly, fig. 13 illustrates pottery of the saucepan pot
continuum which is known to have been in use in Wiltshire and Hampshire in
the third and second centuries, but it too could have continued to be made for
some decades after 100 B.C. All that can safely be said, therefore, is that while

the occupation of Hengistbury in the third and second centuries is possible, it cannot yet be proven. Only further excavation and the discovery of well-stratified groups from the earliest layers will allow the problem to be solved. At the very least it can be said that the pottery evidence would allow that the site was occupied in the second century B.C.

The defensive earthworks (figs. 14–17)

The most prominent feature, representing the Iron Age occupation of Hengistbury, is the system of earthworks which cut off the headland and protected it from landward attack. What now remains is a mutilated and silted remnant of a double ditch and double bank defence of which about a quarter of the original length has been destroyed by coastal erosion. In general overall measurement the defences consist of an inner bank 3 m high and about 14 m wide fronted by a ditch 3·5 m deep and 10 m wide, beyond which was an outer bank, 1·5 m high and 10 m wide and an outer ditch 2 m deep and 6 m wide. The inner ditch has substantially silted up, while the outer ditch is now completely obscured, partly by silting and partly by a thick deposit of blown sand trapped in a dune-like formation against the outer bank (fig. 14).

When Grose observed the earthworks in 1777 he was able to record that both ends were re-curved and that the defensive line was broken by three 'entrances' dividing the earthworks into four sections (fig. 17). By the time that Bushe-Fox had begun his excavations in 1911 most of the southernmost section had disappeared, whilst a new 'entrance' had been cut through the northernmost section at the point where the re-curve began. In all probability the only gap which can claim to be the original Iron Age entrance was the northernmost gap recorded by Grose, immediately opposite the cottage, where the ends of the inner rampart curve inwards. A cable trench dug through the entrance in 1973, observed by John Lavender and Paul Aitken,

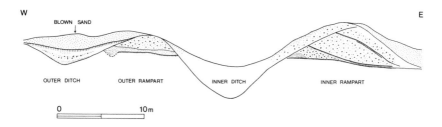

Fig. 14 Section of the double dykes based on the measurements and photographs taken by Bushe-Fox in 1911 when the earthworks were exposed on the southern shore.

Fig. 15 General view of the inner rampart and ditch looking south.
(Photograph: Mike Rouillard)

produced ample evidence of tumbled stonework of the kind which might have revetted an inturned entrance of Iron Age type. Clearly, only by excavation will the form and sequence of the original entrance be revealed. The other gaps in the defences are in all probability post-Iron Age in origin, but cannot otherwise be closely dated.

The northern re-curved end has been much altered in recent times, but originally it would appear that the inner rampart swept round, almost at right angles to its main alignment, to end on the marsh edge, while the inner ditch, here of massive proportions, curved to follow it. The outer defences flank the corner, ending at the marsh, but do not follow the full length of the inner rampart return. The nature of the southern return is recorded only on the small-scale sketch plan which illustrated Grose's description, but the detail is sufficient to suggest that here the inner rampart re-curved along the top of the cliff edge with the outer bank following it, perhaps descending to the shore (fig. 17).

Little is known of the structure and sequence of the defences, but Bushe-Fox was able to photograph and record a nearly complete section, which at that time was exposed along the southern shore, showing that both ramparts were composed of tips of gravel and sand (figs. 14 and 16). The outer rampart appeared to be of one build, but the inner rampart showed evidence of two intermediate turf lines which imply that three phases of construction are represented at this point. Bushe-Fox cut only one partial section of the inner rampart at a point where the stratigraphy suggested that at least two phases of construction were present. In another excavation he established the profiles of both ditches. From what little evidence is at present available, therefore, it would seem that the inner bank was of more than one phase, but no dating evidence of any kind has been obtained. A reasonable hypothesis would be to suggest that the earliest defence was constructed at the time of the earliest Iron Age occupation in the seventh–fifth centuries, perhaps with a refurbishment a few centuries later, the earthworks assuming their present form towards the beginning of the first century B.C., when the site began to be intensively occupied. Once more, excavation is required if the problem is to be settled.

At a distance of some 200 m east of the present double dykes a section of another bank and ditch of defensive character, now totally obscured on the surface by blown sand, can be seen in the cliff section. The bank, 10 m wide at the base, was composed of gravel with a core of turf, possibly representing a marking-out bank. In front, the ditch measured about 7 m wide and 2 m in depth. No dating evidence survives, nor is it evident what course the defensive line took across the promontory. While it is probable that the eastern earthwork wholly pre-dated the double dykes, the possibility remains that it may have been contemporary with an early phase of the double dyke system, the two lines forming part of the same system of defence or enclosure. The problem is incapable of solution on present evidence.

Fig. 16 The double dyke seen in section on the southern shore in 1911. Upper: the inner bank; lower: the outer bank and ditch. Compare with fig. 14.
(Photographs: Bushe-Fox negatives in collection of the Society of Antiquaries)

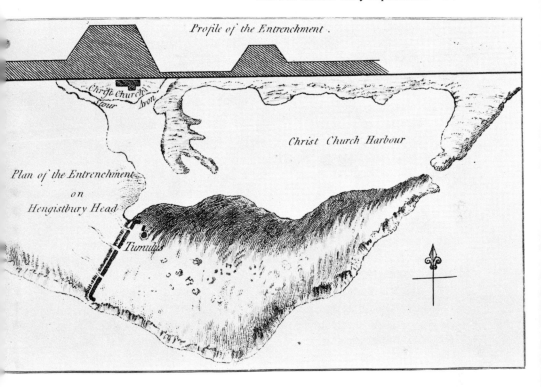

Fig. 17 Plan of Hengistbury taken from Francis Grose, 1779.

2

Trading port and oppidum:
the archaeological evidence

It was in the first century B.C. that Hengistbury assumed the functions of an international trading port, and it is to this period that the bulk of the archaeological finds recovered from the excavations of Bushe-Fox and St George Gray belongs. The range of material is remarkable. The assemblage of pottery, more varied here than from any other Iron Age site in Britain, represents not only local production but trade with the west of England and with north-western France; evidence for metal working and manufacturing industries is plentiful; coins, both local and imported, abound; while a range of luxury objects must reflect a high level of wealth among the inhabitants. Taken together, this evidence leaves little doubt that Hengistbury is one of the most outstanding Iron Age sites in Britain. Its potential in providing a factual basis for understanding the socio-economic structure of late Iron Age society, and the period of dynamic change brought about by a sudden flowering of international trade, cannot be matched.

Having said this, it must be admitted that the evidence available for defining structures and assessing stratigraphy is not good. There are two reasons for this: first, the excavations of 1911–12 and 1918–24 were, for the most part, carried out by means of digging long, narrow trenches and expanding these only when a feature of interest was observed; and secondly, the soil above the natural surface, within which the archaeological material was found, was very sandy and had been subject to wind-blowing and intensive rabbit-burrowing, both processes causing much disturbance of the original stratigraphy. For these reasons it is impossible to re-establish with any degree of assurance groups of associated material from among the old collections. Dr Peacock's trial excavation of 1970, however, showed beyond doubt that by applying modern techniques of excavation, stratigraphical distinctions could be recognized. Thus a programme of large-scale area excavation could reveal not only the plan of part of the settlement, but would also allow the chronological development of the site and its trading patterns to be considered in finer detail than is at present possible.

Bushe-Fox observed a range of structural evidence. Clay floors, possibly

Fig. 18 *opposite* Iron Age gold scrap. Upper: mass of gold as found; lower: the individual pieces extracted.
(Photographs: Bushe-Fox negatives in collection of the Society of Antiquaries)

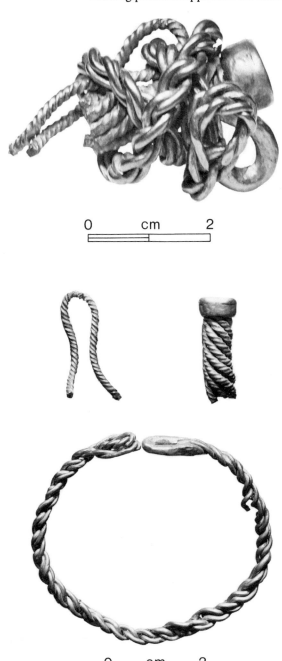

representing houses, were noted at a high proportion of the sites, and several times he recorded the presence of daub showing wattle marks, which may well have come from house walls. On site 16 an oblong clay floor 2·4 by 1·2 m was uncovered with part of an adjacent wall standing to a height of 35 cm, but pottery from above the floor was of Roman date. A fragment of a wattle-and-daub wall on site 58 seems, however, to have been associated only with late Iron Age pottery. Hearths and other evidence of burning were comparatively plentiful. Gullies and small ditches, presumably for drainage purposes, were noted on several sites, including sites 27, 39, 41, 42, 43 and 48, usually in association with pottery which should be dated to the late first century B.C. or early first century A.D. If the impression that drainage gullies were dug only in the last phase of Iron Age occupation is correct, it might reflect a rise in the water table in the decades before the Roman invasion.

Evidence for industrial activity is widespread and deserves detailed consideration.

Manufacturing industries

The Head itself is an important source of good quality ironstone which was extensively mined in the nineteenth century. The readily accessible nature of the ore would undoubtedly have been of considerable benefit to the Iron Age community, and indeed may well have attracted settlement to the site in the first instance. Lumps of ironstone were discovered on sites 15, 18 and 36, while site 4 produced slag from iron working. Green vitreous slag which may also have resulted from iron smelting was recovered from site 11. More recently, John Lavender has noted five small iron-smelting hearths on Warren Hill which, though undated, may well belong to the Iron Age.

More remarkable is the extensive evidence recovered by Bushe-Fox for the working of silver, copper and lead. Since a detailed report on the metallurgical activity was prepared by Sir W. Gowland for the excavation report (Bushe-Fox 1915, 72–83), here we need only summarize the principal conclusions.

The importation of the raw material was represented by two bun-shaped ingots, both from site 33. One, weighing 5 lb 10 oz, proved to be of almost pure copper (98·5%), but the other, which weighed 19 lb 8 oz, was basically a copper-silver alloy composed of 50·45% copper, 46·43% silver and as much as 1·20% gold. Gowland estimated that in this block alone there were over 9 lb of pure silver and nearly $3\frac{1}{2}$ oz of gold! Site 33 also produced a quantity of slag and small pieces of argentiferous copper, which when melted down and analysed as one sample proved to be nearly 68% copper and 30% silver. It would seem likely, therefore, that argentiferous copper was being imported into Hengistbury. Gowland was of the opinion that the alloy may have come from the Callington district of Cornwall, where native silver and silver-copper

Fig. 19 Kimmeridge shale. Scale 1/2. Cores from lathe turnings and hand cutting and fragments of finished objects, including bracelets.
(Photographs: Bushe-Fox negatives in collection of the Society of Antiquaries)

ores are known to have been extracted in historical times. If this were so then the ingot of nearly pure copper could have resulted from a purification process taking place at Hengistbury. It is, however, equally possible that the copper ingot was brought to the site in the state in which it was found, there to be deliberately alloyed with silver and gold.

There is clear evidence that argentiferous copper was being refined to produce pure silver at Hengistbury. Two cupellation hearths were found, one on site 9 and another on site 24. The process of cupellation involved the construction of a sunken hearth, lined with a thick layer of bone ash, within which the alloy was placed together with the charcoal. Heat was then applied to raise the temperature of the metal to melting point. Once the alloy had melted, the charcoal would have been scraped aside to expose the surface of the molten metal. The success of the process depended upon the fact that copper was more rapidly oxidized than was silver. In practice it would have been necessary to add lead, which would immediately have oxidized to form litharge, a substance capable of absorbing the copper oxides. The mixture of oxides would have formed a scum on the surface, which could then have been scraped off or would have been absorbed by the lining of the furnace. As the process continued, so the silver content of the remaining metal increased. If a silver rich alloy was the desired product, the process could be stopped when the silver : copper ratio had reached the required level.

The two cupellation hearths were examined in detail by Gowland. His analyses showed that the linings were composed of bone ash which had absorbed considerable quantities of copper and lead oxides. The small globules of metal found in one hearth contained 16% silver, while those from the other contained 57%. Thus it would appear that some of the argentiferous ore reaching Hengistbury was being refined by cupellation to increase its silver content or to produce the pure metal. The process would have required a considerable quantity of lead, which must have been brought to the site, probably from the Mendips. A few fragments were found in St George Gray's excavations in the Nursery Garden area.

The casting of bronze was also undertaken on site 33. Gowland records an 'ingate', a piece of metal which had solidified in the inlet of a mould. His analysis showed it to contain 88% copper and 9% tin. Another fragment of similar composition was found near by. Gowland was of the opinion that the ingate resulted from the casting of coins on the site (below p. 44). Blobs of once-melted bronze, together with bronze slag and a crucible which had been used for melting bronze, were also noted by St George Gray in the Nursery Garden area (fig. 30, no. 13).

Gold may also have been worked on the site. Site 33 produced a small gold bracelet, part of a torc and another fragment all twisted together as though they represented a collection of scrap (fig. 18), while a stone of siliceous shale from site 7 was identified by Gowland as a touchstone streaked with marks which indicated that it had been used for testing gold.

Two other activities carried out at Hengistbury required the importation of raw materials: the manufacture of armlets of Kimmeridge shale, and glass working. Kimmeridge shale, from the Dorset coast, was brought to the site in quantity both as raw blocks of quarried shale and as large beach pebbles. Two processes were used in the Iron Age to produce armlets: hand cutting and lathe turning. Waste material from both has been found at Hengistbury (fig. 19). The nature of the glass-working activity is more difficult to assess. Both Bushe-Fox and St George Gray discovered several lumps of crude purple glass of a type which had been coloured with manganese salts and contained a high percentage of tin. In all probability these fragments had been imported from the continent, their presence suggesting that glass beads and bracelets were being manufactured locally, perhaps on Hengistbury itself. It may be

Fig. 20 *opposite* Durotrigan coins from Hengistbury. Scale 1/1.
1, 2　Durotrigan C, struck staters.
3–10　Durotrigan D, cast staters.
11, 12 Durotrigan E, thin silver.

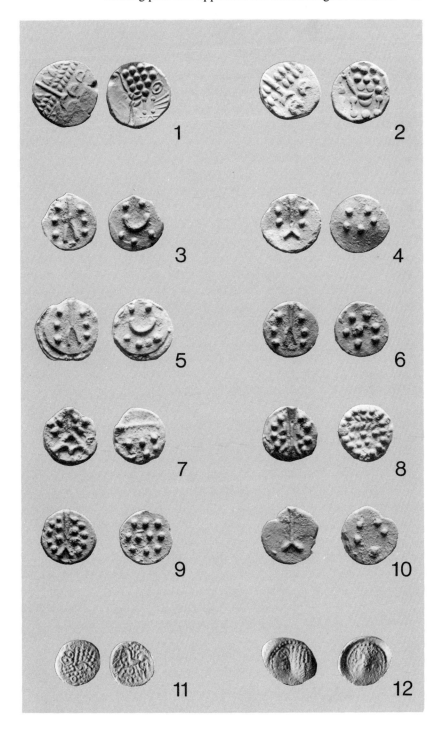

significant that among the finished glass objects found on the site were two fragments of purple-coloured bracelets.

So far we have said nothing of the date of these activities, for the simple reason that no good dating evidence exists. All the sites from which the evidence quoted above was derived, produced quantities of Late Iron Age pottery, while some yielded Roman sherds. While, therefore, a Roman date for some of these activities is possible, the general paucity of Roman material from the excavations would argue strongly in favour of an Iron Age date somewhere in the bracket 100 B.C.–A.D. 43.

Coins and the problem of the mint

Much of the evidence for metal working comes from site 33, an area which also produced the bulk of the coins found on Hengistbury. Gowland believed that coins were minted here, a view accepted by several later writers, but as Derek Allen has pointed out, there is no shred of indisputable evidence to show that this was so (Allen 1968, 55, n.2). Clearly the area is of crucial significance, but unfortunately stratigraphical and structural evidence is wanting. Bushe-Fox described the site, some 8–10 m across, as consisting of 'the remains of a dwelling or dwellings . . . of a most fragmentary character' represented by an irregular patch of clay and gravel with ironstone blocks scattered about immediately adjacent to a layer of burnt clay and stones set at a higher level: 3 m or so to the south was a shallow depression cut into the natural soil. The soil, the excavator records, was riddled with rabbit burrows and had been further disturbed by ploughing. In other words, no reliable stratigraphy was recorded and finds, potentially of widely differing dates, had probably been churned up together. Within this restricted area were found more than 3,000 coins, of which 1,660 were cast bronze issues of the Durotriges (Durotrigan uninscribed D) and 1,308 were struck bronze (Durotrigan uninscribed C) (fig. 20), more than 100 were Roman ranging in date from Republican issues to those of Antoninus Pius, and a handful of others included Gaulish and British issues (Appendix C, pp. 86–9). The collection has been variously interpreted. Bushe-Fox hinted at the possibility that it was a dispersed hoard, a view which Allen was inclined to accept, but close consideration of the evidence, such as it is, suggests that this need not be the case. Evidently the coins had been deposited in separate bundles, perhaps wrapped in an organic material. One bundle, consisting of 743 coins, had been carefully placed on a stone with two stones on either side, giving the impression that the group had not been disturbed. A second bundle, comprising 281 coins, which had corroded together to form a cylindrical mass, was found 6 m away. Strictly these two groups should each be regarded as separate hoards. The first contained 607 cast coins (Durotrigan D), and 126 struck varieties (Durotrigan C), while the second hoard was made up largely of cast types of which 278 were identified. No Roman coins were found in either of these groups. Bushe-Fox describes the rest of the collection in these words:

Several other smaller lumps of coins were also found. In some cases these consisted of coins of similar types unmixed with other varieties. Such lumps consisted of specimens of the Hengistbury type [i.e. Durotrigan D], the south-western type [i.e. Durotrigan C], Roman denarii (generally in too decomposed a state to identify), or Roman bronze. Many of the coins were in pieces when found, and a larger number were in too bad a condition to lift out of the soil; others fell to pieces after being taken out of the ground.

If the view is taken that all the coins were deposited at one time, then one must accept that quantities of Durotrigan coins were still in circulation in the middle of the second century A.D.; if, however, the possibility is allowed that deposition took place over a period of time, then the bulk of the Durotrigan coins could have been lost or buried before the Roman conquest. The archaeological evidence from site 33 does not allow a firm conclusion to be reached.

In considering the dating of Durotrigan coins, Allen (1968, 54–6) concluded that the bronze struck staters were in full development by A.D. 43 and were still in use in A.D. 86, and that the bronze cast staters were not demonstrably in existence before A.D. 86, but continued in circulation at least up to c. A.D. 110. The evidence for this dating rests partly on the Hengistbury deposit just described and partly on a hoard found at Holdenhurst in 1905 (Hill 1911). This hoard, buried in a Roman vessel and probably deposited within the reign of Hadrian (A.D. 119–38), contained a remarkable collection of coins which included 17 Roman denarii ranging in date from the late second century B.C. to Vitellius, 44 Imperial asses from Agrippa to Hadrian and 616 Celtic coins, mostly of the Durotriges, of which 206 were struck bronze and 406 were cast bronze. Clearly the collection represents an accumulation which could have been brought together over a period of time. Whilst *allowing* that the Durotrigan issues were in circulation in the second century A.D., the hoard cannot be taken to *prove* the fact. In other words there is no indisputable evidence yet available to show that the cast and struck Durotrigan bronze coins were being minted after the conquest. A closer study of the coins themselves may eventually throw more light on this vexed problem.

Allen was correct in pointing out that there was no reason to *assume* that coins were minted on Hengistbury Head, but when the scraps of evidence are considered together it must be allowed that minting *may* have taken place. We have seen that cupellation was being undertaken, which is in itself suggestive, while in the area of the coin finds on site 33 (an area of barely 40 square

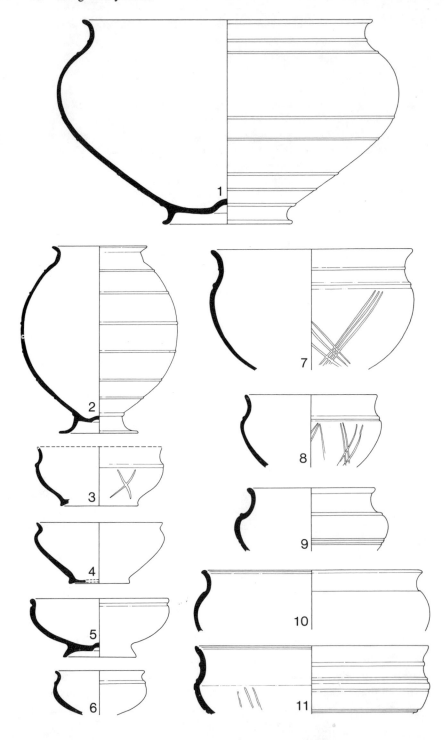

metres) there was found scrap gold, a copper ingot, an ingot of silver-copper alloy, and a casting ingate of a composition similar to that of the cast bronze coins. The range of evidence is suggestive if not conclusive.

Imported and local pottery

One of the most significant aspects of the archaeological collection from Hengistbury is the large and varied assemblage of pottery which has been amassed as the result of the various excavations. There are three principal collections (the first two of which must be regarded as unstratified): that made by Bushe-Fox and selectively published by him in 1915; the St George Gray collection, unpublished and stored in the Red House Museum, Christchurch; and the material obtained by Dr Peacock in 1970, which is at present being prepared for publication. In view of Peacock's work, which will include a detailed fabric analysis, the discussion here will be brief.

Bushe-Fox, writing at a time when very little was known of Iron Age pottery, divided the material into twelve classes which he designated A to L. Class A included a range of types which we would now date to 700–400 B.C., while class K and some vessels of his class L are of Roman date. The rest belong to the period *c.* 100 B.C.–A.D. 50: of this, classes B, C, E, F, G, H and some of L constitute a range of types which seem to be largely restricted to the Hengistbury neighbourhood, Class D includes contemporary types imported from south-western Britain, whilst much of the pottery listed under classes I and J together with some of class L typifies the assemblage in use in Dorset and adjacent areas in the century or so before the Roman conquest: these types are commonly referred to as Durotrigan (Brailsford 1958). For ease of discussion, therefore, we will divide the Late Iron Age pottery into the *Hengistbury assemblage* and the *Durotrigan assemblage*, and to avoid

Fig. 21 Pottery of class 1, black cordoned ware. Scale 1/4.
1 Brown sandy ware with black burnished surface (after Bushe-Fox 1915, pl. XVII, 3).
2 Fine hard grey ware with highly burnished black surface (B.-F. M. Col.).
3 Brown sandy ware with black burnished surface (SGG. Red House Mus.).
4 Brown sandy ware with black burnished surface (SGG. Red House Mus.).
5 Grey sandy ware with highly burnished black surface (SGG. Red House Mus.).
6 Grey sandy ware with black burnished surface (SGG. Red House Mus.).
7 Grey sandy ware with highly burnished black surface (B.-F. Brit. Mus.).
8 Brown sandy ware with highly burnished black surface (SGG. Red House Mus.).
9 Greyish-brown sandy ware with black burnished surface (SGG. Red House Mus.).
10 Brown sandy ware with black burnished surface (SGG. Red House Mus.).
11 Grey sandy ware with highly burnished black surface (SGG. Red House Mus.).

confusion with Bushe-Fox's classification the Hengistbury assemblage will be subdivided into seven numbered classes. These classes are at best only a broad categorization which, when the material has been studied in more detail, will be capable of subdivision into a number of different fabric and form types.

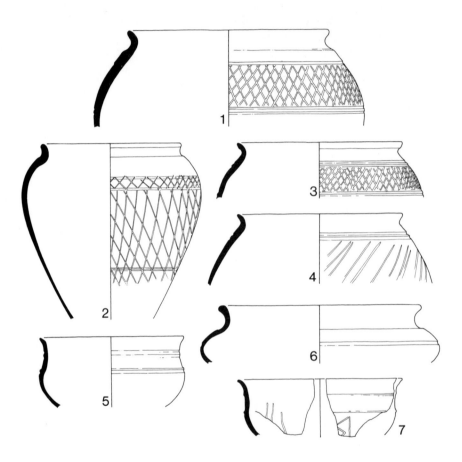

Fig. 22 Pottery of class 2, graphite coated ware. Scale 1/4.
1 Coarse grey sandy ware. Graphite coated external surface (B.-F. Brit. Mus.).
2 Graphite coated vessel (after Bushe-Fox 1915, pl. XXII, 7).
3 Grey sandy ware. Graphite coated external surface (SGG. Red House Mus.).
4 Coarse grey sandy ware. Graphite coated external surface (SGG. Red House Mus.).
5 Grey sandy ware. Graphite coated external surface (SGG. Red House Mus.).
6 Grey-brown sandy ware. External coat of graphite down to shoulder (SGG. Red House Mus.).
7 Brown sandy ware. External coat of graphite to just below shoulder and internally over lip (SGG. Red House Mus.).

The classic Hengistbury assemblage

Class 1 wares (fig. 21)

Class 1 vessels, perhaps the best known of the Hengistbury pottery, can be equated directly with Bushe-Fox's class B. All vessels were wheel-turned and were frequently decorated with cordons and also sometimes with burnished lines on the lower part of the bodies. Invariably they were finished to a high standard with fine black burnished surfaces. The range of forms is restricted to wide open-mouthed bowls, jars, and small bowls of varying profile, all usually with well-formed pedestal and omphalos bases.

At least two distinct fabrics can be recognized: a fine hard grey ware and a somewhat coarser brown sandy ware, suggesting the possibility of at least two centres of production. Though rare in Britain the general class is known in Normandy, Brittany and the Channel Islands, and there can therefore be little doubt that it was distributed as the result of cross-channel trade. Until the fabric analyses have been completed it is difficult to be more precise, but it remains a possibility that the vessels made in the fine grey ware are imports, while the brown sandy fabrics may represent locally-made copies.

Class 2 wares (fig. 22)

Class 2 is equivalent to Bushe-Fox's class H, which is characterized by the use of graphite to decorate the surfaces of vessels. The forms can be divided into three general types: jars with external lattice decoration, wide-mouthed bowls with neck cordons, and shouldered bowls of varying forms. While the jars seem to have been coated with graphite all over the external surface, the bowls were usually coated only on the rim and shoulder. The fabric varies slightly, but is usually sandy and fired to a grey or brown colour.

Like class 1 vessels, these graphite-coated wares are rare in Britain and at present are known only from the Hengistbury and Poole Harbour regions, but they occur in Normandy, Brittany and on Jersey and Guernsey. In all probability they were made in northern France and were transported to Britain by sea.

Class 3 wares (fig. 23)

This group was not clearly distinguished by Bushe-Fox, but includes some of the vessels which he illustrates as class L. It is characterized by small bowls with deep rilled decoration usually on the shoulder but sometimes extending down to the lower part of the body. The fabric is usually, though not invariably, sandy and heavily micaceous, and is fired to a grey or brown colour. The micaceous wares could not have been locally made, but in the absence of detailed fabric analyses a place of origin cannot be defined. Rilled wares, though extremely rare in southern Britain, are known on a number of

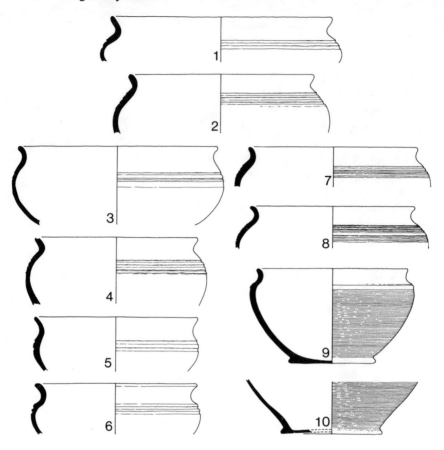

sites in north-western France, whence some of the Hengistbury vessels may well have been imported.

Class 4 wares (fig. 24)

This class includes all the vessels which are generally called by the general purpose term 'Glastonbury ware' and which Bushe-Fox categorized as his class D. Peacock's recent study of Glastonbury ware (Peacock 1969) has shown that the general style can be divided into six groups based on fabric definition, each of which represents a different area of production in the west of England. Of the five Hengistbury examples which Peacock examined, three belonged to his group 1, which was made from clay found only in the Lizard peninsula of Cornwall, one belonged to group 2, which included grits derived from the Old Red Sandstone of the Mendip region, and one belonged to group 6 tempered with grit from the Permian outcrops of Devon. Bushe-Fox records

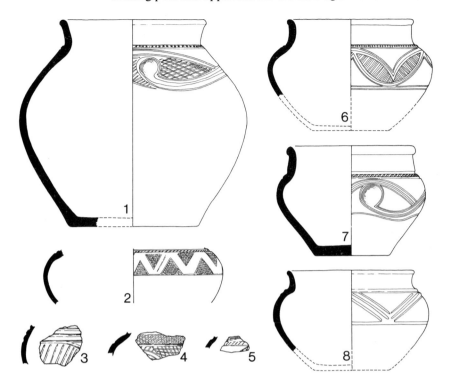

Fig. 23 *opposite* Pottery of class 3, rilled micaceous ware. Scale 1/4.
1 Grey sandy ware fired reddish-orange; micaceous (B.-F. Red House Mus.).
2 Grey sandy ware fired grey; micaceous (B.-F. Red House Mus.).
3 Coarse black sandy ware fired red on the surfaces (B.-F. Red House Mus.).
4 Coarse brownish sandy ware fired black (B.-F. Red House Mus.).
5 Fine grey sandy ware with burnished micaceous surface (B.-F. Red House Mus.).
6 Coarse brown sandy ware with burnished micaceous surface (B.-F. Red House Mus.).
7 Grey sandy ware; micaceous (B.-F. Red House Mus.).
8 Fine grey-brown sandy ware; micaceous (B.-F. Red House Mus.).
9 Gritty micaceous ware (after Bushe-Fox 1915, pl. XXVI, 9).
10 Black sandy ware (B.-F. Red House Mus.).

Fig. 24 Pottery of class 4, Glastonbury ware. Scale 1/4.
1 Fine black sandy ware with black burnished surface (B.-F. M. Col.).
2 Grey-brown ware with limestone grit tempering. Black burnished surface (?B.-F. Red House Mus.).
3 Smooth grey ware with black burnished surface (SGG. Red House Mus.).
4 Brown ware with (?) limestone grit tempering. Black burnished surface (SGG. Red House Mus.).
5 Grey ware with (?) limestone grit tempering (?B.-F. Red House Mus.).
6 Hard grey ware with white grits. Brown surface (after Bushe-Fox, 1915, pl. XX, 4).
7 Light-grey ware with dark angular grits (B.-F. M. Col.)
8 Dark-grey ware with grey-brown burnished surface (after Bushe-Fox, 1915, pl. XX, 3).

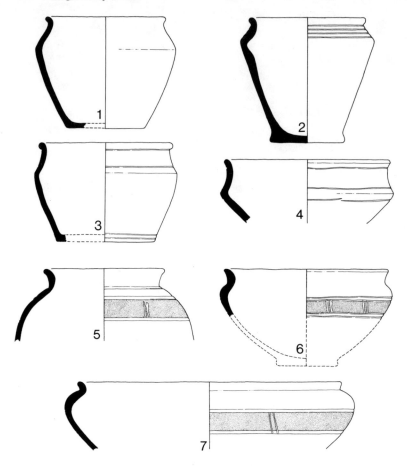

Fig. 25 Pottery of classes 5 and 7. Scale 1/4.
Vessels of class 7.
1 Grey sandy ware with burnished surface (B.-F. M. Col.).
2 Soft grey-brown ware with burnished surface (after Bushe-Fox, 1915, pl. XIX, 1).
3 Grey sandy ware with black burnished surface (B.-F. M. Col.).
4 Soft grey ware with burnished surface (B.-F. Brit. Mus.).
Vessels of class 5.
5 Hard grey sandy ware (after Bushe-Fox 1915, pl. XXI, 2).
6 Hard grey sandy ware (B.-F. Brit. Mus.).
7 Hard grey sandy ware (B.-F. Brit. Mus.).

that about a dozen vessels were represented altogether, to which two more
can be added from the St George Gray collection. Two of the vessels not
sampled by Peacock (fig. 24, nos. 1 and 7) are typologically very similar in
form and decoration to examples of group 1. If they prove to be so, then at
least one-third of the Hengistbury sample would be of Cornish origin.

Significantly, it is this group which has the most widespread distribution in southern Britain.

Class 5 wares (fig. 25)

This is equivalent to Bushe-Fox's class G. It represents a small group of vessels including bowl and jar forms made in a hard grey sandy ware and decorated distinctively with horizontal zones, defined by grooves between which the surface of the vessel is slightly roughened, contrasting with the rest of the surface, which is burnished. The group is numerically small and is at present restricted in distribution to Hengistbury.

Class 6 wares (fig. 26)

The group defined here as a single class includes Bushe-Fox's classes E and F, which differ only in their styles of decoration. For the most part the vessels are jars with upright or everted rims, made in a smooth soapy fabric fired grey to black and burnished on the surface. Decoration, which is generally restricted to the shoulder, can be divided into two styles: one is dependent upon the use of hemispherical indentations, usually contained within horizontal zones; the other uses the roulette wheel to impress patterns ranging from simple linear designs to more complex compositions incorporating Greek key patterns, arcs and wave motifs. This class is virtually restricted to Hengistbury, and is in all probability of local manufacture. The pottery forms and the range of decoration are reminiscent of vessels of the Late Iron Age found in Essex, Kent and Sussex, and are perhaps best seen simply as a local variation within a widely distributed general style.

Class 7 wares (fig. 25)

Class 7 is broadly equivalent to Bushe-Fox's class C. The forms include a range of shouldered jars and bowls with simple bead rims, sometimes with shallow grooves on the shoulder or neck. The fabrics vary, but are usually of sandy type and fired grey or black. Outside Hengistbury the type is poorly represented in Britain (one example occurs at Maiden Castle), but is fairly common in northern France and the Low Countries. A cursory examination of the fabrics would suggest that the Hengistbury examples were locally made.

In summary, it may be said that of the seven major classes which constitute the classic Hengistbury assemblage, three, classes 1, 2 and 3, represent imports from northern France, together perhaps with their local copies, class 4 includes material imported from the west of England, class 6 was locally produced essentially in a native tradition, while classes 5 and 7 were probably made locally but under continental inspiration.

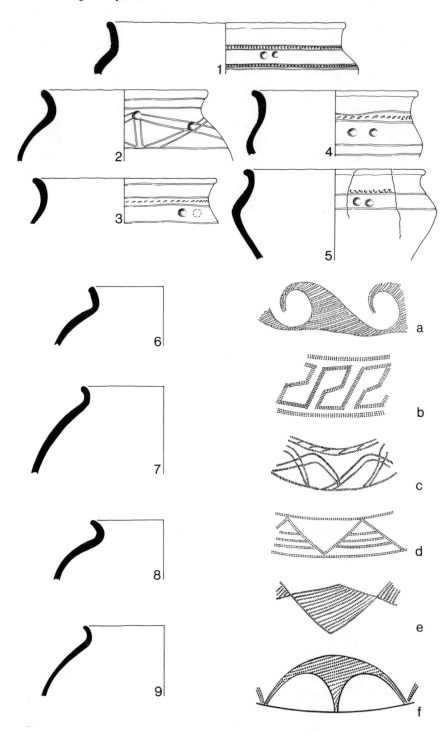

Internal dating evidence from Hengistbury is sparse and unreliable. Suffice it to say that pottery of all seven classes was frequently found in association and was seldom noted to occur with Durotrigan wares of Bushe-Fox's classes I and J. Sir Mortimer Wheeler's excavations in northern France, particularly at Le Petit Celland (Manche) and Le Camp D'Artus (Finistère), demonstrated beyond reasonable doubt that classes 1, 2 and 3 were in use in northern France in the decades immediately preceding the Caesarian conquest. On this evidence alone the importation of these wares is most unlikely to have taken place after 56 B.C., and more probably represents trade in the 70s and 60s of the first century. The range of possibilities was neatly summed up by Wheeler when he concluded that the foreign pottery at Hengistbury could be 'the relics of a few ship-loads of refugees at the time of the Caesarian conquest. They may, on the other hand, be commercial products of a somewhat earlier date' (Wheeler and Richardson 1957, 47).

The importation of wine

That Hengistbury was involved in widespread trade with the continent in the first half of the first century is vividly demonstrated by the evidence provided by the amphorae found on the site, which has recently been considered in some detail by Dr Peacock (1971, 173). Peacock was able to show that the collection contained at least twelve Italian amphorae, of a form known as Dressel IA, which was in common use in the first half of the first century B.C. (fig. 27). Not only is Hengistbury outstanding in the quantity of this type which it has yielded, but only two other sites in Britain, Green Island in Poole Harbour and Knighton, Isle of Wight, have so far produced indisputable examples of vessels of this kind. The implication must surely be that the port was in direct contact with the shippers of Italian wine. Moreover, the variety

Fig. 26 *opposite* Pottery of class 6. Scale 1/4.

1 Coarse grey ware with limestone (?) grits. Burnished black surface (B.-F. Red House Mus.).
2 Smooth grey ware with burnished surface (B.-F. Brit. Mus.).
3 Smooth grey ware with sparse grits. Roughly burnished surface (SGG. Red House Mus.).
4 Smooth grey ware with sparse limestone (?) grits. Roughly burnished surface (SGG. Red House Mus.).
5 Smooth grey ware, burnished surface (B.-F. Brit. Mus.).
6 Smooth grey ware. Burnished surface, decorated with rouletted pattern d (B.-F. Brit. Mus.).
7 Smooth grey ware. Burnished surface decorated with rouletted pattern (B.-F. Brit. Mus.).
8 Smooth grey ware. Burnished surface decorated with rouletted pattern c (B.-F. Brit. Mus.).
9 Smooth grey ware. Burnished surface decorated with rouletted pattern (B.-F. Brit. Mus.).

a–f are examples of rouletted patterns used to decorate jars of types 6–9 (after Bushe-Fox 1915, pl. XXI).

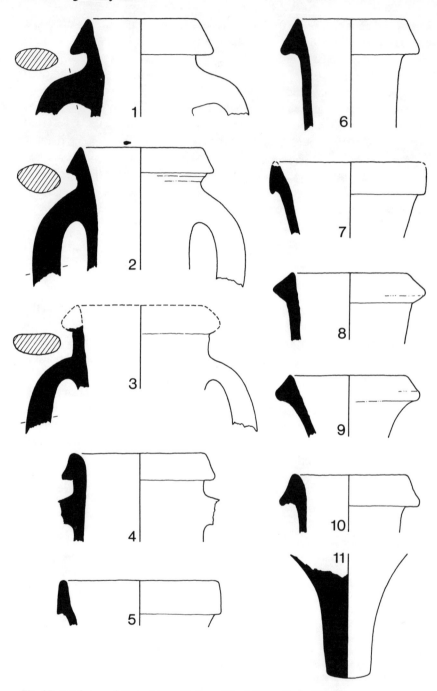

Fig. 27 Amphorae of Dressel type IA from Hengistbury. Scale 1/4.
(After Peacock 1971, fig. 37)

of rim types discovered suggests that a number of different cargoes are represented.

The Durotrigan assemblage and later imports

The excavations at Maiden Castle and at a number of other Iron Age sites in Dorset have brought to light an assemblage of pottery which is now well recognized as representing the pottery of the Durotriges in the last century or so before the Roman conquest. The forms have been defined and discussed by Brailsford (1958), who has recognized twelve major types, principally bowls and jars. The majority of these types have been found at Hengistbury, and a selection is illustrated here (fig. 28).

Durotrigan pottery is usually well-made and wheel-turned. The origins of most of the types can clearly be seen in the local ceramic tradition of the preceding centuries, which has been categorized as the Maiden Castle–Marnhull style (Cunliffe 1974, 44–5), the principal differences being brought about by the introduction of the potter's wheel. Two of Brailsford's Durotrigan types (his nos. 10 and 11) cannot, however, be related to earlier local prototypes. Both no. 10, a cordoned tazze form, and no. 11, a shouldered bowl with neck cordon, are, however, similar in form to Hengistbury class 1 pottery, from which types they were no doubt derived. In other words, the simplest explanation for the evolution of the Durotrigan assemblage would be to suppose that it developed out of the indigenous ceramic tradition strongly influenced by the improved technology which was introduced into the Hengistbury region in the first half of the first century B.C. If this is so, then the fully formed Durotrigan assemblage cannot have come into existence until after c. 50 B.C. Such an explanation conforms well with the available dating evidence.

At Hengistbury, though generally widespread, Durotrigan pottery was concentrated in the ditches found on sites 39, 48 and 51. The ditch of semi-circular plan found on site 48 was particularly informative for it provided a well-stratified sample of Durotrigan pottery associated with imported terra rubra and terra nigra platters, Arretine ware and sherds of a Gallo-Belgic girth beaker. Sealing the ditch was a large oval 'oven' (site 49) measuring 1·2 by 0·8 m. Bushe-Fox records that its walls were stengthened with potsherds and that the filling contained a quantity of pottery (of Durotrigan type) burnt red. It is possible that the 'oven' may, in fact, have been a pottery kiln, but the contention is difficult to prove. The occurrence of the Gallo-Belgic platters and beakers, and also of the supposed Arretine sherd, would suggest a date in the early first century A.D. for the sealed group, although a decade or so earlier would not be impossible.

Imported Gallo-Belgic and Italian pottery is not common at Hengistbury

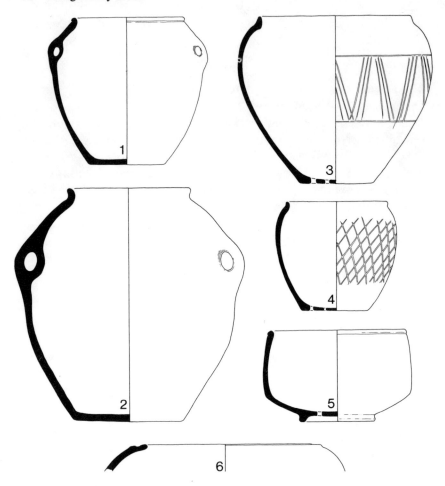

Fig. 28 Durotrigan pottery. Scale 1/4.
1 Grey sandy ware (after Bushe-Fox 1915, pl. XXIV, 27).
2 Grey sandy ware (after Bushe-Fox 1915, pl. XXIV, 22).
3 Hard grey sandy ware. Black burnished surface (after Bushe-Fox 1915, pl. XXIII, 5).
4 Hard brown ware. Burnished (after Bushe-Fox 1915, pl. XXIII, 8).
5 Hard dark grey ware, darker grey slip (after Bushe-Fox 1915, pl. XXIII, 13).
6 Hard light grey ware (after Bushe-Fox 1915, pl. XXVI, 7).

and those fragments which are recorded need not have arrived before the period of the Claudian conquest in A.D. 43. The virtual absence of Dressel type IB amphorae, widespread in south-east Britain in the period 50 B.C.–A.D. 50, strongly suggests that extensive trading systems comparable to those of the pre-Caesarian period were no longer in force at Hengistbury after Caesar's conquest of Gaul (below pp. 78–9).

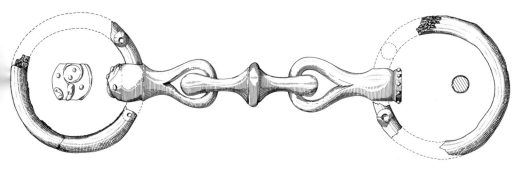

Fig. 29 Bridle bit. Scale 1/4.
The rings, now much corroded, are of iron cased with sheet bronze, upon which traces of finely chased decoration are just visible. Each had a pair of stop knobs riveted on. The mouth piece is bronze. The ends of the side links are differently ornamented: one is domed and decorated with curved strokes and dots in high relief; the other is dished to take an inset of glass or enamel, now missing, held in place by an iron pin. The rim of the casting is simply decorated with pellets in relief. That the ends bear different decoration suggests that the bit was one of a pair. (SGG. Red House Mus.)

Luxury objects (figs. 29 and 30)

The excavations have produced an interesting range of small objects which reflect upon the standard of living of the occupants. The most impressive are undoubtedly the fragments of gold and silver torcs found on site 33. One of these finds consisted of a twisted mass of gold which when untangled proved to represent two objects, one complete and one fragmentary. The complete object was a small torc composed of twisted strands of gold wire fashioned in such a way that one terminal was looped, the other being formed into a solid disc. Its diameter, 7·5 cm, would suggest use as an armlet. The fragmentary object comprised the terminal and part of one strand of a larger torc, with a plain buffer terminal, made up of multiple strands of twisted gold rod wound together. Near by, on site 33, another object was found, which at the time was thought to be the head of a linch-pin in silvered bronze. It is, however, the cast terminal of a large torc (fig. 30, no. 7) which analysis has shown to have been made of silver which originally seems to have been gilded (Clarke 1954, 64, n. 4).

This collection is of particular interest since the state of the objects, and indeed the context in which they were found, implies that by the time of deposition they were regarded as scrap metal, probably collected together to be melted down. The Hengistbury torcs belong to a well known class of objects widely distributed in the British Isles, particularly in East Anglia, and

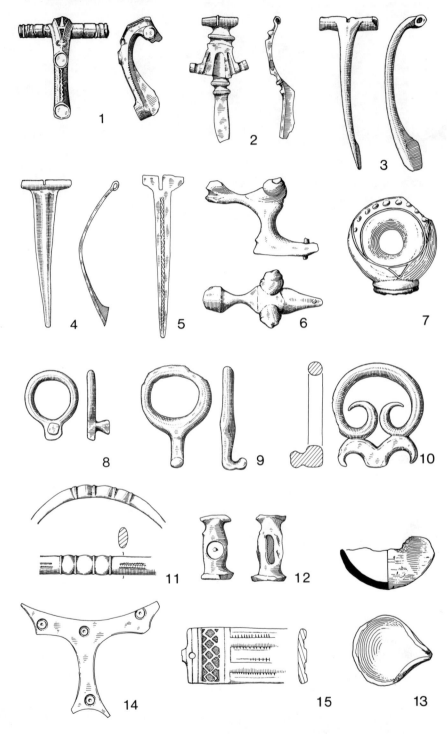

broadly dated to the first century B.C. (Cunliffe 1974, 283–4). Where they were made, whether in a single workshop or at a variety of locations, is still uncertain.

A number of other objects of copper alloy have been found (fig. 30). No. 6 is of particular interest: it is a small bronze casting in the form of an animal head with bulging eyes, which had been riveted to another object. The creature is evidently a bird of some kind, possibly a duck. Parallels are difficult to find, but a naturalistic rendering of a duck was found in a Late Iron Age context at Milber Down, Devon. In style, however, particularly the treatment of the swelling nose, the Hengistbury animal is much closer to the ox-heads found at Ham Hill, Somerset, and Dinorben, in north Wales, both of which should be dated to the first century B.C. or first century A.D. Although ducks are

Fig. 30 Small objects. Scale 2/3, except for no. 13, which is 1/3.

1   Bronze brooch of T-form with hinged pin and enamel inlay. A Dorset type occurring at Hod Hill, Dorchester, Woodcuts and Rotherlay (Bushe-Fox 1915, pl. XXIX, no. 4 for incomplete drawing, before conservation. Brit. Mus.).
2   Bronze brooch of Hod Hill type (SGG. Red House Mus.).
3   Bronze brooch of simple form with hinged pin. Comparable to the 'dolphin' type (*Camulodunum type V*) (SGG. Red House Mus.).
4   Bronze brooch with hinged pin. Langton Down type (*Camulodunum type XII*) (SGG. Red House Mus.).
5   Bronze brooch with hinged pin and flattish bow, probably derivative of *Camulodunum type XVIII* (SGG. Red House Mus.).
In addition to the brooches illustrated here Bushe-Fox (1915, pl. XXIX) illustrates a bronze brooch of Deal type (no. 1) and two iron Nauheim derivatives (nos. 2 and 3).
6   Zoomorphic fitting in bronze apparently in the form of a bird, once riveted to another object (Bushe-Fox 1915, pl. XXIX, no. 6, Brit. Mus.).
7   Terminal of a silver torc, once gilded (Bushe-Fox 1915, pl. XXX, no. 13 for incomplete drawing before conservation. Brit. Mus.).
8   Bronze ring from chain belt: La Tène III type (Bushe-Fox 1915, pl. XXIX, no. 8. Brit. Mus.).
9   Bronze ring catch from chain belt: La Tène III type (Bushe-Fox 1915, pl. XXIX no. 7. Brit. Mus.).
10 Bronze harness fitting (Bushe-Fox 1915, pl. XXX, no. 14. Brit. Mus.).
11 Bronze bracelet fragment (SGG. Red House Mus.).
12 Bronze toggle-like object of uncertain use (Bushe-Fox 1915, pl. XXIX, no. 9. Brit. Mus.).
13 Crucible bearing traces of bronze working (metal residue identified by Professor E. T. Hall of the Research Laboratory for Archaeology and the History of Art, Oxford) (SGG. Red House Mus.).
14 Handle of a bronze vessel, probably a wine strainer of La Tène III type, well known on the Continent. For recent discussion of the type see Chapotat 1970, 85–8 (Bushe-Fox 1915, pl. XXIX, no. 11, for drawing before conservation. Brit. Mus.).
15 Bronze bracelet fragment with enamel inlay (found on north shore of Hengistbury in 1952, Red House Mus.).

frequently depicted in Early Iron Age (Hallstatt) contexts on the continent, the style of the Hengistbury beast is more in keeping with the spirit of British art of the later Iron Age.

Another object of note is the fine three-link horse bit found by St George Gray in 1920 (Ward Perkins 1939, 191) (fig. 29). It is one of a comparatively small group of such items which demonstrate not only the high degree of technical skill achieved by the craftsmen of the first century B.C., but also the desire of the owners of such pieces to display their wealth.

Of the other objects of copper alloy illustrated here, no. 14 is part of a handle attachment of a bronze vessel, no. 9 is probably a hook belonging to a chain belt of which no. 8 may also be a part, while no. 10 is a decorative attachment possibly for a horse harness. All can be widely paralleled on the continent in Late Iron Age contexts. The assemblage is completed by a range of brooches in copper alloy and iron, bracelets of copper alloy, and shale and glass beads, all representing the personal jewellery of the inhabitants.

Taken together, the collection is notable not only for its range but also for its quality. The impression it gives is of a level of wealth well above that displayed by contemporary farming settlements, a fact further emphasized when the imported coins are taken into account. The luxury objects, imported pottery and manufacturing activities together show that in the Late Iron Age Hengistbury was a settlement of far more than local importance. That it was an urban community engaging in long-distance trade cannot be doubted. It remains now to consider the site in its broader historical and economic context.

3

Hengistbury as a port of trade

In the previous chapter, we surveyed the archaeological evidence for occupation and activity on Hengistbury in the period from about 100 B.C. until the time of the Roman invasion in A.D. 43. It now remains to discuss that evidence in the light of the dramatic cultural and economic revolution which Britain was undergoing at the time and to examine what part, if any, Hengistbury played in this process of change.

Before we can begin to approach the question it is necessary to look briefly at the nature of Iron Age culture in central southern Britain in the centuries leading up to 100 B.C. For the most part the landscape was densely settled by small communities practising mixed farming in a traditional manner which seems to have changed little for over a thousand years. Some modifications to the farming regime, such as the development of winter sowing, had been introduced and no doubt careful breeding had over the years improved the stock, but the picture is essentially one of stability and continuity rather than of change. One new factor, however, can dimly be detected—it would seem that the population had begun to grow significantly by the third and second centuries.

Most of the people lived in individual farmsteads or in small villages, but a growing proportion occupied the many hillforts which are densely distributed over the Wessex landscape. The idea of enclosing a hill top for defensive reasons can be traced back for centuries to about 1000 B.C., but it is only after the middle of the first millennium that regular occupation on any scale can begin to be detected. From this time onwards there is clear evidence that some hillforts became the centres of large territories, averaging 40 square miles or so in extent, and that they were subjected to continuous refurbishment of an increasingly defensive nature. In all probability these hillforts provided a range of services for the rural communities which were dependent upon them—services which would have included provision of protected storage, facilities for the redistribution of goods and products from the hinterland, and for long-distance trade in non-local products, and also perhaps some degree of control over the religious, legal and administrative aspects of community affairs (Cunliffe 1976, 138–41).

Evidence from the large-scale excavations at Danebury, a hillfort 50 km north of Hengistbury, shows that here, by the second century B.C., was based a large resident population, the members of which, in addition to undertaking farming pursuits, were working imported bronze, iron and Kimmeridge shale, were probably engaged in marketing salt brought in from the Solent shores in briquetage containers, and may well have been manufacturing pottery. The order apparent in the layout of streets and buildings and the massive nature of the defences implies a degree of sustained coercive control by a central power (Cunliffe 1977). In other words, these developed hillforts had, by the second century B.C., acquired a number of functions not unlike those we would expect of an urban centre. To class the developed hillforts as 'urban' would, however, be to go beyond the reasonable limits of the evidence. Rural-based activities still seemed to dominate the life of the inhabitants, and the number of resident specialists employed in full-time non-agricultural pursuits must have been very small. Thus, while there can be little doubt that the hillforts were essential to the efficient social and economic functioning of Iron Age society, and each served to coordinate everyday life in its territory, it is best to regard them as the precursors of full urban development.

Little can be said of Hengistbury in this period. It is probable, however, that the defensive earthworks were already in existence, if not in their final form, and a sufficient group of local pottery has been found (Maiden Castle–Marnhull style) to allow the possibility of occupation in the second century. Although the evidence is sparse it may be that, at this time, Hengistbury performed a similar range of functions to the developed hillforts of Wessex.

It was in the first century B.C. that the old socio-economic order was suddenly disrupted. Over most of Sussex, Hampshire, and parts of Wiltshire, hillforts were abandoned wholesale, although the rural settlements continued to be occupied apparently without disruption. In place of the hillforts there is evidence to suggest that new defended enclosures were being built, often on valley sides in positions ideal for controlling major river crossings. The implications would seem to be that in the east of the region the long established hillfort-dominated system was being replaced by a different type of social and economic organization in which command of trade routes was a prime concern (Cunliffe 1976, 145–9). In the west, however, in Dorset and parts of Somerset and Wiltshire, the old hillforts continued in use and indeed were still in good defensive order at the time of the Roman conquest in A.D. 43 and 44, when Vespasian, commanding the Second Legion, overcame more than twenty of them. Wheeler's excavation at Maiden Castle and Richmond's work at Hod Hill provide vivid evidence of hillfort life in the last decades of the pre-Roman Iron Age (Wheeler 1943; Richmond 1968).

Superimposed upon these regional differences it is possible to recognize a sudden increase in contact between the south-east of Britain and the adjacent continent after several hundred years of relative isolation. Pottery technology improved and continental types were widely copied, fashions displayed in continental jewellery were eagerly taken up and the volume of imports, including coins and luxury goods such as wine and high quality table ware, dramatically increased. Whatever the immediate cause or causes of this change (below pp. 77–8), increased contact on this scale with the continental world would have demanded a reorientation of trading methods leading to the development of an organized market economy. A money system was soon adopted to facilitate exchange, and by the time of the Roman invasion a full-scale urban society had come into being in the south-east of the country. Hengistbury lay on the fringe of this later development, but there is compelling evidence to suggest that in the initial stages the port played a crucial role in the opening up of southern Britain to continental traders.

Hengistbury as a production centre

The evidence outlined in Chapter 2, with all its chronological imprecision, vividly demonstrates that Hengistbury was a production centre for a wide range of commodities. Production was of two kinds: the exploitation of locally occurring materials and the refining of, and manufacturing from, substances imported into the site in their raw state.

Hengistbury was particularly rich in mineral resources. The headland was composed of good quality iron ore readily accessible without mining, simply by the collection from the shore of lumps which had eroded out of the cliff. There can be little doubt that the iron was extracted on a large scale and would have been a major attraction to settlement. Good potting clay could be had near by at Wick marsh and from the slopes of Warren Hill, and, though difficult to prove, it seems probable that pottery was being manufactured on the site; nor is it likely that the inhabitants would have overlooked the northern shore as a convenient area for salt production.

The list of non-local products is even more impressive: lead probably from the Mendips, argentiferous copper from Cornwall, copper possibly from Devon and Cornwall, shale from the Dorset coast, manganese glass probably from continental Europe, and scrap gold collected together from inland locations. The shale was worked on site to make armlets, while the glass may also have supplied local craftsmen engaged in the manufacture of beads and bracelets. Since no evidence of working has been found, however, it remains a possibility that the glass slab was traded in its raw state.

The metals pose an interesting series of questions. While the copper cake, together with the crucible and droplets of metal, need imply little more than the casting of decorative and domestic objects, and the scrap gold could have been used simply as currency or may have been intended to have been refashioned into torcs, the extraction of silver from argentiferous copper implies a different order of working. It may well be that the silver was used for the local manufacture of coins, but it could equally well have been intended for export, perhaps to Armorica where silver coinage was in wide circulation. Whether or not Hengistbury became a mint in its later years is a vexed question, to which there can yet be no firm answer.

The existence of such a wide range of imported raw materials implies that an extensive pattern of contact had been established, particularly within the West Country (fig. 31). This is borne out by the discovery, at Hengistbury, of pottery of 'Glastonbury' style manufactured in three separate centres in Cornwall, Devon and the Mendips—just those areas from which the metals were imported. Whether or not trading links existed with Wessex or the south-east it is more difficult to say. A few pottery vessels of central Hampshire type have been found, but nothing more. It is, however, possible that products of the kind which would have left no archaeological trace were being exchanged. The absence of south-eastern material from the site finds does not in itself

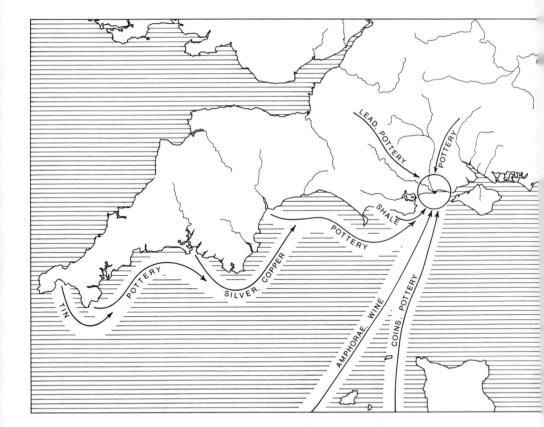

Fig. 31 Hengistbury and its trading contacts. Showing in diagrammatic form the possible routes along which non-local commodities reached the site.

imply a lack of contact. If, however, the coin list is considered, it is surely significant that, in addition to large quantities of Durotrigan coins, Hengistbury has yielded more than thirteen coins of the Dobunni, whose territory lay in Gloucestershire and Somerset, but none of the Atrebates or of the other tribes in the south-east. The coin evidence, therefore, supports the impression given by the other archaeological material that the British trade links of Hengistbury were principally with the metal-producing communities of the south-west.

Long-distance trade

As a port for overseas shipping, Hengistbury had obvious advantages. It lay directly opposite the Cherbourg peninsula and was thus the shortest crossing between Atlantic France and Britain—a journey of only 110 km, which could have been accomplished in twelve sailing hours in good weather. Moreover, the promontory is easily recognizable from the sea and, once rounded, ample sheltered anchorage could be found in its lee.

The most impressive evidence for long-distance trade at Hengistbury is undoubtedly provided by the large collection of Italian amphorae, principally of Dressel IA type (see above p. 55), which Peacock has suggested must represent many cargoes of wine delivered to the port in the first half of the first century B.C. The apparent absence of these early amphorae in Armorica (with the exception of a collection found on the site of a shipwreck off Belle Île, south of the Morbihan) might suggest that the wine trade between Italy and Britain was, at least in part, direct. If so, it is tempting to see the Belle Île wreck as a Roman merchant ship which foundered en route to Britain.

The sheer quantity of Dressel IA amphorae from Hengistbury, which far exceeds that from all the other southern British sites put together, leaves little doubt that the site was the principal port of entry into the country, where the cargoes of wine would have been off-loaded for distribution to inland sites. That other ports may also have been in use is, however, hinted at by the discovery of amphora fragments on Green Island in Poole Harbour, and another from Weymouth Bay, though these could equally well have been transported thence by British coasters operating from Hengistbury.

Once unloaded, the foreign ships would presumably have taken on a cargo of British produce for the return journey. Strabo, writing at the beginning of the first century A.D., indicated the range of goods available when he said that Britain 'produces corn, cattle, gold, silver, iron. All these are exported together with hides, slaves and dogs useful for hunting.' As we have seen, all these metals were being produced or refined at Hengistbury, while the other products could easily have been brought in from the Wessex hinterland. Although, of course, Strabo was writing of Britain in general, and at a later

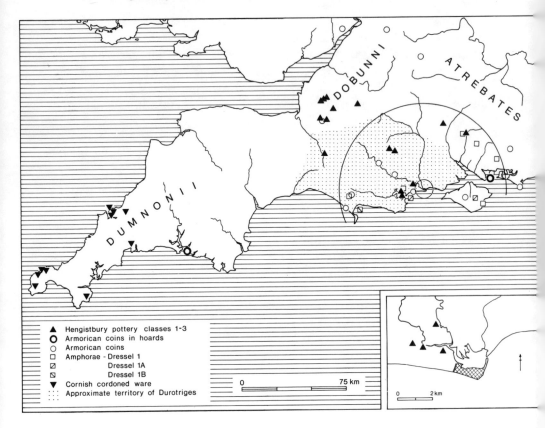

▲ Hengistbury pottery classes 1-3
◉ Armorican coins in hoards
○ Armorican coins
□ Amphorae - Dressel 1
▨   Dressel 1A
▨   Dressel 1B
▼ Cornish cordoned ware
∴ Approximate territory of Durotriges

0   75 km

0   2 km

date, his account does at least indicate the range of commodities which would
have interested the foreign traders putting in at Hengistbury. Elsewhere he
lists four ports of origin commonly used by trading missions. Of these the
mouths of the Loire or the Garonne would seem the most likely starting points
for expeditions to the Hengistbury region. A route from the Mediterranean,
via the Garonne to the Atlantic, would have allowed the traders to cut out the
long sea journey which would otherwise have taken them around the Iberian
peninsula.

Direct contact with north-western France is amply demonstrated by the
considerable volume of imported pottery of French origin found at
Hengistbury and in the immediate neighbourhood (fig. 32). The three classes
of imported wares, black cordoned vessels, graphite coated fabrics and the
rilled micaceous wares, are all widely distributed in Brittany and to a lesser
extent in Normandy (fig. 33). French archaeologists generally agree that
vessels of this kind belong to 'La Tène finale', while excavations carried out by

Fig. 32 *opposite* The distribution of commodities imported through Hengistbury and related types.
Coin distribution is after Allen 1961 with additions, the distribution of amphorae after Peacock 1971. The Cornish cordoned ware is based on various sources. The sites shown as producing Hengistbury class 1–3 pottery are as follows:

Inset map   Mill Plain (classes 1 and 2)
              Burleigh Road (class 1)
              Tuckton Farm (class 1)
              Wick (class 1)

50 km radius   Red Hill Common, Bournemouth, Dorset (class 1)
              Hamworthy, Dorset (class 2)
              Green Island, Poole, Dorset (class 2)
              Woodcuts, Dorset (class 1)
              Rotherby, Wilts. (class 1)
              Danebury, Hants. (classes 1 and 3)
              Winchester, Hants. (class 1)

Beyond 50 km Wookey Hole, Somerset (class 1)
              Coopers Hole, Cheddar, Somerset (class 1)
              Car Park, Cheddar, Somerset (class 1)
              Glastonbury, Somerset (class 1)
              Meare, Somerset (class 1)
              Kings Down Camp, Somerset (class 1)
              Ham Hill, Somerset (class 1)

Many vessels which resemble those of class 1 but are in coarser fabrics have been omitted. Those listed here as class 1 conform in type and fabric (on visual inspection only) to types found at Hengistbury.

Wheeler (Wheeler and Richardson 1957) and Threipland (1945) have shown these types to have been in use in hillforts during the last stages of Gaulish independence. In spite of the comparatively large number of findspots shown on fig. 33, the French assemblages are neither extensive nor well known; indeed it is fair to say that more imported La Tène pottery has been found at Hengistbury than from all the listed French sites taken together. For this reason detailed discussion is unwise, especially with so little pottery yet recorded from Normandy (for summary of Iron Age finds see Bertin 1975). Superficially, however, it would appear that the black cordoned wares (class 1) have a more easterly distribution (Ille-et-Vilaine, Manche and Calvados), than the graphite coated (class 2) and micaceous (class 3) wares, which are found mainly in Côtes-du-Nord, Finistère and Morbihan. The two distributions overlap in the Côtes-du-Nord and Ille-et-Vilaine region, hinting at the possibility that north coast ports in the St Malo and Le Mont St Michel region may have been involved in the cross-channel traffic—a suggestion which gains further support when the coin distributions are considered (fig. 35 and below pp. 73–4). The occurrence of imported wares at several locations

Fig. 33 *opposite* Distribution of selected La Tène III pottery types in north-western France and Britain.

British sites: see caption to fig. 32.

Channel Islands: Mont Orgueil, St Martins, Jersey
                  Maîtress Ile, Minquiers, Jersey
                  La Hougue au Compte, Câtel, Guernsey
                  Les Issues, St Saviour, Guernsey
                  Catioroc, St Saviour, Guernsey

France:

1 Petit Celland, Manche (Wheeler and Richardson 1957).
2 Camp d'Artus, Huelgoat, Finistère (Wheeler and Richardson 1957).
3 Ile Gaignog, Landéda, Finistère (Giot and Bourhis 1964).
4 Stang-Vihan, Concarneau, Finistère (Le Roux 1967).
5 Kermoysan, Plabennec, Finistère (Le Roux and Lecerf, 1973; Le Bihan and Galliou 1974).
6 Kercaradec, Penhars, Finistère (Wheeler and Richardson, 1957).
7 Tronoën, Port l'Abbe, Finistère (Wheeler and Richardson, 1957).
8 Kersigneau, Plouhinec, Finistère (Wheeler and Richardson 1957).
9 Kervédan, Ile de Groix, Morbihan (Threipland 1945).
10 Plouhinec, Port Louis, Morbihan (Threipland 1945).
11 Pointe du Vieux Château, Belle-Île en Mer, Morbihan (Threipland 1945).
12 Saint-Jude en Bourbriac, Côtes-du-Nord (Briard and Giot 1963)
13 Villers sur Mer, Calvados (Caillaud and Lagnel 1964).
14 Saint Malo-d'Alet, Ille-et-Vilaine (Sanquer 1975).
15 Moulin-de-la-Rive, Locquirec, Finistère (Giot, Deunff, Briard and L'Helgouach 1958).
16 Bellevue, Plouégat-Moyson, Finistère (Giot, Le Roux and Onnée 1968).
17 St Donan, St Brieuc, Côtes-du-Nord (Giot, Lecerf and Onnée 1971).
18 Grève des Rosaires, Plérin, Côtes-du-Nord (Giot, Lecerf and Onnée 1971).
19 Bourg, St Glen, Côtes-du-Nord (Giot, Lecerf and Onnée 1971).
20 Rugére, Plouvorn, Finistère (Giot, Lecerf and Onnée 1971).

on the Channel Islands of Jersey and Guernsey gives some further indication of the routes which the trading vessels might have taken.

Although the imported pottery has been found in great quantity at Hengistbury, it does not appear to have been widely distributed elsewhere in Britain. Four sites in the immediate neighbourhood have produced these wares, to which may be added a further seven within 50 km of Hengistbury. The only significant distribution beyond this limit is the cluster of findspots in the Mendip region which, as we have already seen, was linked to Hengistbury by other categories of traded goods.

Apart from the sites close to Hengistbury, the other locations shown (fig. 32) have each yielded only one or two examples of black cordoned wares, and these, though stylistically close to imported types, may, on analysis, prove to be locally made derivatives.

The importance of the north-western French imports was not so much their

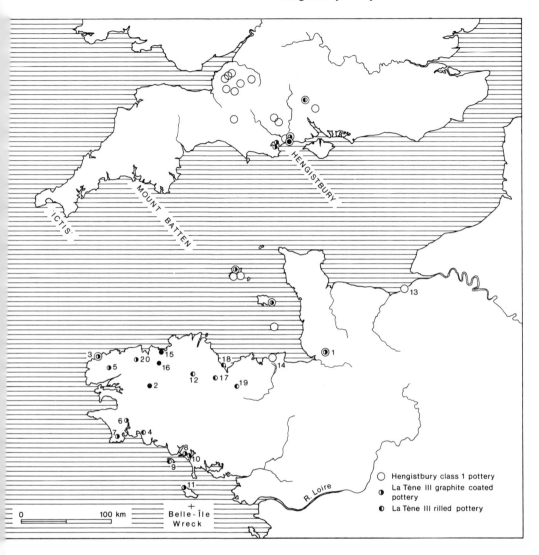

O   Hengistbury class 1 pottery

◑   La Tène III graphite coated pottery

◑   La Tène III rilled pottery

wide distribution, but the effect that the improved technology, which they represent, seems to have had on local ceramic development. If we are correct in assuming some of the types to have been copied locally at Hengistbury, then this would represent the earliest use of the potter's wheel in southern Britain. It is a distinct, but unproven, possibility that immigrant potters actually settled at Hengistbury to exploit the new markets which were opening up at the time. This newly introduced commercialism would seem to lie at the beginning of the Late Iron Age ceramic developments of the Durotriges in

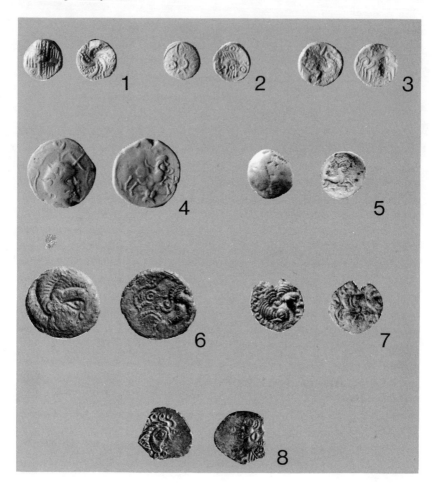

Fig. 34 Armorican coins from Hengistbury. Scale 1/1.
1 British/Gaulish D.
2 British/Gaulish E.
3 British/Gaulish F.
4, 5 Namnetes.
6, 7 Coriosolites.
8 Abrincatui.

Dorset and the Atrebates in Hampshire in the last hundred years before the Roman invasion.

A further indication of trade with north-western France is provided by the coin evidence (fig. 35). Hengistbury has produced no less than 25 imported coins, of which 21, certainly, and 4, probably, originate in Normandy and Brittany (fig. 34). The Namnetes of the Loire mouth region are represented by two coins, the Abrincatui of Manche by two, their neighbours the Baiocasses of Calvados by one, while the Coriosolites and Osismii of northern Armorica are between them represented by at least sixteen coins (Appendix C). Excluding the hoard and other finds from Mount Batten (which is itself of considerable importance as an Iron Age trading port) the Hengistbury collection accounts for about 40% of the total Armorican coins known in Britain. Thus the coin evidence, like that of the pottery, emphasizes the peculiar nature of the port and underlines its close links with north-western France. The recent discovery of a gold 'bullet' coin of Gallo-Belgic XB type may hint at a tenuous contact with the Aisne or Marne area of northern France.

Exchange of coins seems to have been essentially one-way. Apart from the famous Le Catillon hoard in Jersey only one Durotrigan coin is at present known in France, significantly in Calvados. It should, however, be remembered that the Armorican coins were minted before Caesar's conquest of north-west Gaul in 56 B.C. They may well have arrived in Britain at a time largely before local British coinage had begun to develop.

Several classical writers provide explicit accounts of long-distance trade with Britain. We have already discussed the list of exports provided by Strabo in his general remarks about Britain as a whole. Most of the other sources are concerned with the tin trade. Herodotus, writing in the middle of the fifth century, mentions the 'Cassiterides, from which our tin comes' (iii, 115), but the earliest source is a lost Massilian account of a voyage undertaken in the sixth century, loosely quoted in the poem *Ora Maritima* written by Avienus in the fourth century A.D. Although such second-hand and embroidered information is likely to be unreliable in detail, we can accept the general basis of his remarks, namely that a group of islands, called the Oestrymnides, which lay off the coast of Brittany, were rich in tin. One possibility is that it was British tin which was brought to these islands for collection by Mediterranean traders. Some support for this view may be sought in Timaeus, the Sicilian historian (quoted in a garbled version by Pliny, *Natural History* iv, 30, 16), when he refers to an island called Mictis, six days' distant from Britain, 'in which tin is produced, and that the Britons sail to it in vessels made of wickerwork covered with hide'. The meaning of the account is, to say the least, ambiguous. It could (just) be taken to imply that tin was brought from Britain to an island trading post six days' sailing away, but it would seem more reasonable to take it as meaning that tin was carried from an area, thought to be an island, and to which the name Mictis was attached, six days by boat to Britain. If this were so, one possible interpretation is that coastal contact existed between the tin-producing areas of the south-west (Mictis), which had the appearance of being an island, to more familiar ground known to be Britain, there presumably to be collected by traders.

A more straightforward account (contradicting the last) is provided by another Sicilian writer Diodorus (V, 22), possibly quoting an older source by Pytheas. Diodorus refers to a part of Britain called Belerion (probably the Land's End peninsula) where, he says, the natives were used to trading with foreigners. It was here that tin was extracted and turned into ingots shaped like *astragli* (knuckle-bones), which were transported to an off-shore island, Ictis, which could be reached only at low tide. 'Here the merchants buy the tin from the locals and take it to Gaul, and after travelling overland for about thirty days they finally bring their loads on horses to the mouth of the Rhône.' Thence the tin was taken to Narbonne and Marseilles. This account implies direct trading between south-west Britain and the Mediterranean, a view which is further reflected in the words of Strabo (III, 147, quoting Poseidonios *c.* 90 B.C.) who says that 'tin was carried from the British Isles to Marseilles'. (The identification of Ictis as St Michael's Mount, Cornwall, and a consideration of the texts which mention it, has recently been discussed with full references by Maxwell, 1972.)

From these various accounts it is evident that the tin trade was of vital importance and that it was in operation at least by the sixth century B.C. Much of the trade, like that bringing wine to Britain, appears to have been direct, but the possibility remains that intermediate trading ports may also have been used, sited perhaps off the Breton coasts and in parts of Britain more readily accessible to traders. That Breton middle men were probably involved in at least some of the transactions is suggested by Caesar's description of the Veneti, whose territory lay on the southern coasts of the Armorican penin-sula, as a maritime nation who were accustomed to sail to Britain (*B.G.* III, 8). Strabo went so far as to assert that 'they were ready to stop Caesar from sailing to Britain, in as much as they enjoyed the trade' (IV, 194). It is tempting to see them transporting the Cornish tin to Corbilo at the mouth of the Loire whence, either overland via the Loire or by further boat trips along the coast to the Garonne, it was taken to the Mediterranean coastal ports.

Clearly, the trading patterns were complex and interwoven, and it is beyond the scope of the archaeological and literary evidence for the true situation ever to be fully appreciated. Having admitted this, however, the following systems may reasonably be isolated:

(1) direct trade between Cornwall and the Mediterranean world involving Mediterranean traders;

(2) direct trade between Cornwall and the Mediterranean world involving the Veneti in transporting goods to the Loire mouth where Mediterranean traders would take over;

(3) indirect trade, the tin being taken to off-shore Breton islands by British ships;

(4) indirect trade, the tin being taken to a British port, such as Mount Batten or Hengistbury, for collection and transshipment.

What part, if any, Hengistbury played in this trading complex it is impossible to be sure. Its links with Cornwall, demonstrated by the presence of group 1 Glastonbury ware, are indisputable, but no direct evidence of the tin trade has yet been recovered from the site. By the time that Hengistbury rose to prominence early in the first century B.C., tin trading was an old-established system, and it is possible that the emergence of the new port had little effect on it. It is, however, difficult to believe that the development of such an important trading station, optimally sited for easy contact with the continent, would not have deflected existing patterns and drawn to itself at least a share of the tin trade. It may even be that the improvement in pottery techniques evident in Cornwall, at the time which saw the development of wheel-made 'cordoned ware' (Threipland 1956), was in some way inspired by contact with the Hengistbury pottery industry. These speculations, while inherently possible, cannot yet be substantiated.

Chronology, history and explanation

It is necessary now to consider two separate but interrelated problems: the development of Hengistbury as a port-of-trade and its significance in its wider historical context. Both tasks are difficult, not least because of the virtual absence of reliable stratigraphical evidence from the site itself, and the comparative lack of relevant contemporary documentation. Nevertheless, the broad historical framework is clear, and against this the archaeological evidence can be set.

The works of the various classical writers mentioned above leave little doubt that in the first half of the first century B.C. the tribes of Armorica had established close and friendly trading relations with their neighbours in southern Britain. The situation would, however, have been seriously disrupted by Caesar's conquest of Gaul and in particular by the uprising of the Veneti of 56 B.C., as the result of which Caesar moved into north-western France in force, destroying the Venetic navy, slaughtering and enslaving a substantial body of the population and annexing the entire territory for Rome. Events of

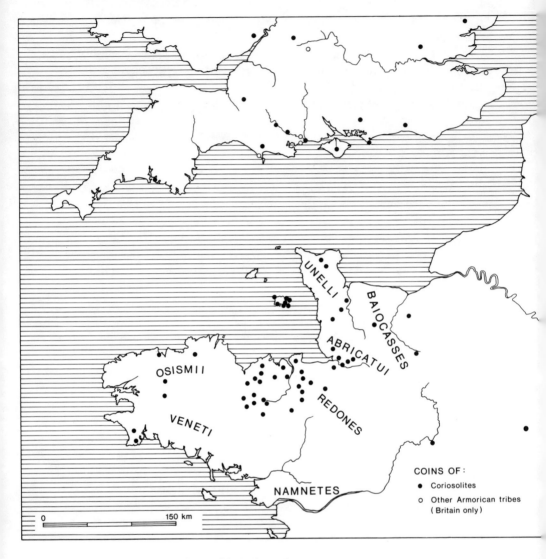

Fig. 35 Distribution of selected Armorican coins.

The British distribution is based on Allen 1961 with additions. The French distribution of coins of the Coriosolites is taken from Colbert de Beaulieu 1973, fig. 33.

this magnitude cannot have failed to have had far-reaching effects on old-established patterns of cross-channel contact.

It is interesting to compare the archaeological material from Hengistbury against this background. The imported Italian amphorae are particularly revealing, since Peacock has been able to show that most of them are of

Dressel IA type, which date largely to before 50 B.C. The IB form, which is more typical of the period 50 B.C.–A.D. 50, is virtually absent from Hengistbury, even though it occurs commonly in other parts of south-eastern Britain. The implication would therefore seem to be that the wine trade with Hengistbury ceased towards the middle of the first century B.C., possibly with the onset of Caesar's campaigns. Other classes of evidence support the idea of a widespread breakdown in trade at about this time. The imported north-western Gaulish pottery, which occurred in quantity at Hengistbury, is known to have been in use in hillforts in Normandy and Brittany, which are themselves unlikely to have been allowed to continue in use after Caesar had annexed the area. While this does not, of course, prove that all the imported types reached Hengistbury before 56 B.C., it is highly likely that Gaulish pottery production underwent significant modification after the Roman conquest. The types found at Hengistbury are without romanizing features. The coins suggest a similar picture (figs. 34 and 35). Armorican coins, particularly those of the Coriosolites, are relatively common at Hengistbury. Since they are unlikely to have been minted after the Roman occupation of Gaul began, they most probably reached the port before, or soon after, the conquest. Thus, taken together, the archaeological evidence supports the view that the lively trading relations which linked Hengistbury to the continental world in the first half of the first century B.C. were drastically curtailed in the middle of the century, as a result of Caesar's annexation of Gaul.

Hengistbury must now be considered in its broader context. During the first century B.C. the communities of south-eastern Britain suddenly, after a period of relative isolation, developed close contacts with adjacent parts of the continent. This is particularly well demonstrated by the appearance, over much of the south-east, of fine quality wheel-made pottery (known after the type sites of Aylesford and Swarling) which developed locally under the inspiration of northern French wares. At the same time Gallo-Belgic coins found their way into Britain, soon to serve as a basis for the evolution of local coin production, while Mediterranean-inspired bronze work, associated with the wine-drinking ritual, now began to make its appearance. Taken together with the evidence from Hengistbury it is clear that those parts of coastal Britain which lay within easy reach of the continent began to develop a material culture closely comparable to that of their cross-channel neighbours. Two principal zones of contact can be recognized, the Hengistbury–Armorica axis, and the Essex/Kent–Belgica axis, which together represent the two shortest sea crossings.

Why this dramatic invigoration of trade should have taken place between Britain and the continent some time about or soon after 100 B.C., after several centuries of relative separation and isolation, is an intriguing and difficult question. No monocausal explanation will suffice, but one factor which must have had a far-reaching effect was the emergence of an urban society in central Gaul. The establishment of a Greek trading port at Marseilles in about 600 B.C. marked the beginning of town development along the northern Mediterranean coast—a development which, within the next few centuries, was to spread to native settlements in Provence. The implantation of the Roman socio-economic system in southern France must have given a new impetus to the development of an urban economy and a state system in hitherto barbarian areas of central Gaul. Trends in this direction were already dimly observable early in the first century, and by the 60s well-developed cities had come into existence among the Arverni and Aedui (for a general discussion of these matters see Nash 1976).

The increasing Roman presence in the south must have dislocated the trading patterns in the surrounding areas, and there can be little doubt that Caesar's campaigns in Gaul in the 50s would have added to the turmoil. In this brief period of rapid change, from c. 100 to 50 B.C., it would not have been surprising if the tribes of northern Gaul, particularly those occupying the maritime areas, had been forced to readjust their traditional trading networks in order to seek new outlets for their products as well as new sources of raw materials for their own use and, perhaps more important, for sale to the avid Roman merchants who were now flocking into the native trading centres. In other words, the opening up of the British markets to continental entre-preneurs in the first half of the first century B.C. can be interpreted as a direct result of the gradual Roman annexation of Gaul.

The completion of Caesar's conquest of Gaul in 51 B.C. marks a significant turning point in relations between Britain and the continent. In the period of rapid romanization that followed, the Gaulish economy would have been adjusted towards, and integrated with, that of the Empire, while trade with barbarian lands like Britain would have come under the control of the government. These changes clearly had a significant effect on Britain. As a generalization it may be said that while long-distance trade between the tribes of south-eastern Britain and the Roman world continued to flourish, there is little to suggest that the markets of the south-west maintained their previous levels of contact. The evidence of the amphorae would appear to demonstrate this point with clarity. The Dressel IB type, which is thought to have become common only after the middle of the mid first century B.C., is found widely in the south-east of the country (Rodwell 1976, 237–43) but is extremely rare in the south-west. Similarly, the other imports, such as Gallo-Belgic pottery, which began to arrive in Britain in late Augustan times, are little known in pre-Roman contexts outside the south-east.

The clear impression given by this evidence is that the south-western markets were deliberately shunned by Roman traders. Why this should be so is a matter of speculation, but the explanation must surely be political rather than purely economic. One possibility is that following Caesar's expedition to Britain treaties were concluded with the south-eastern tribes (the Trinovantes and possibly Catuvellauni) which included monopoly rights in trading, Roman merchants being forbidden to deal except with allies. Some such explanation would conveniently fit the known facts. It would suppose that the mineral wealth of the south-west was channelled through middle men like the Dobunni, and perhaps along the Thames valley, to the east coast ports, those controlling the trade routes sharing in the wealth which was generated.

The long-term effects of this divide were considerable. While the south-east developed a full-scale urban economy leading to the abandonment of hillforts and the emergence of large oppida, of which Camulodunum is a prime example, the socio-economic system of the south-west remained little changed. Long-established hillforts, which represented the old social order of tribal fragmentation, were still in active use in A.D. 43–4 when Vespasian led the Second Legion against the hostile communities west of the Salisbury Avon.

The demise of Hengistbury's overseas trade after the middle of the first century B.C. does not necessarily imply that the settlement declined. It would still have provided a convenient market centre serving to link the Dumnonii with the Durotriges, since coastal transport would have been far more efficient than overland routes, while the rivers Stour and Avon gave easy access to the Wessex hinterland. The coin evidence would suggest that contact was also maintained with the Dobunni in Somerset and Gloucestershire, but the complete absence of the dynastic coinages of the Atrebates, Catuvellauni and Trinovantes at Hengistbury, and indeed their scarcity in the south-west as a whole, could be taken to imply that the respective trading systems of the south-east and south-west were by now mutually exclusive.

Thus in its second major phase, 56 B.C.–A.D. 43, Hengistbury would seem to have taken on a more restricted role, serving as a market for the south-west of Britain. It is possible that it was in this later phase that the principal manufacturing functions developed—functions including the casting of bronze and the extraction of silver. Its inhabitants may also have been involved in producing pottery in the Durotrigan style. Only future excavation will elucidate the true nature of this Late Iron Age settlement. At any rate, its status was still sufficiently high to attract a limited range of imports such as Gallo-Belgic and Arretine(?) pottery, though this may well have been obtained through British middle men, perhaps indirectly via the east coast ports.

The most tantalizing problem posed by the Late Iron Age finds is whether or not Hengistbury served as a mint for the Durotriges in the decades preceding the Roman conquest, turning out vast quantities of cast and struck bronze coins to serve as small change in day to day transactions. On balance the archaeological evidence would favour the view that it was a mint, though the matter is still in dispute. From a purely economic point of view, however, it would have been surprising if a site performing the range of functions evident at Hengistbury had not been provided with minting facilities.

The settlement was still in operation, and may indeed have been actively defended, when Vespasian led his army of conquest through the territory of the Durotriges in A.D. 43–4.

The Roman aftermath

That Hengistbury continued to be occupied in the Roman period is not in doubt, but the nature of the occupation is uncertain. Structural evidence is restricted to a rubbish pit some 3 m deep on site 29, a circular patch of gravel 6 m in diameter on site 35, an area of burnt clay and stones on site 47 and a few isolated hearths in the Nursery Garden area. The discovery of Roman pottery, usually in the topsoil, showed, however, that occupation was spread over an area of about 300 m extending along the north shore of the promontory.

Some indication of the date range of this occupation is given by the coin sequence. Though difficult to prove, the impression is that two distinct phases are represented, the first extending from the Flavian to the Antonine period, the second from the late third to the beginning of the fourth century. Site 33 was particularly prolific of coins. Omitting Republican denarii, 36 of the 43 identifiable coins belong to the period Vespasian–Antoninus Pius, the remainder (including five denarii of Augustus–Tiberius and one bronze each of Augustus and Claudius) could well have been current in this period. While it must be admitted that the evidence from site 33 is slender and confused, the lack of pre-Flavian issues might be significant, suggesting renewed activity in the late first century after a period of abandonment. Of the six other coins from Hengistbury pre-dating the mid third century, four belong to the Flavian–Antonine period.

Whether or not the site remained in continuous occupation throughout the first three-quarters of the third century, fourteen coins dating within the range 270–335 show that occupation continued into the first decades of the fourth century. The absence of later fourth-century issues could imply abandonment. How extensive the late settlement was it is impossible to say, but site 35 was evidently occupied at this time and St George Gray records late material in his Nursery Garden area excavations.

In general the pottery bears out the evidence of the coins. The samian pottery and mortaria date almost entirely to the Flavian–Antonine period, while there is a consistent group of later third- and early fourth-century pottery, particularly from sites 19 and 35, which includes a range of products from the New Forest kilns.

On the surviving evidence, therefore, it would seem that a community occupied the site from the late first to early fourth century, perhaps re-establishing itself on the old occupied area after a period of abandonment following the Roman conquest of A.D. 43. No structures or objects were discovered to suggest that it was anything more than a peasant settlement composed of slight timber buildings, relying for its livelihood on farming, fishing and perhaps the extraction of salt.

When and why the site was abandoned are unknown. No evidence for Saxon use has been recorded on the headland, but by the late ninth century the potential of the harbour was once more utilized, when Alfred, reorganizing the defences of Wessex, constructed a 'burgh' on a site which was destined to become Christchurch, leaving Hengistbury an abandoned but picturesque bastion against the ravages of the sea.

Appendix A
The present location of the archaeological material

The rich collection of archaeological material from the various excavations at Hengistbury has become somewhat dispersed, although all the major items are readily available for study. The following list indicates the whereabouts of the material that can now be traced. The coins are discussed in Appendix C.

Herbert Druitt Collection, 1906–40. The large collection of surface material, mainly flints, amassed by Druitt particularly after the ploughing of 1913, is now in the Red House Museum, Christchurch.

The Bushe-Fox excavations, 1911–12. The Bushe-Fox collection has been split. The principal objects, including the barrow groups, the gold torc fragments, a selection of the coins, the quern stones, and a number of the more complete pots which have been reconstructed, are in the collection of Sir George Meyrick at Hinton Admiral. The British Museum holds a selection of the coins, all the small finds other than those in the Meyrick collection, and much of the pottery, while a selection of pot sherds is housed in the Red House Museum. Collections of coins were donated to a number of museums (see pp. 86–9).

The St George Gray excavations, 1918–24. Most of the material, except for some of the Bronze Age pottery (now unlocated), is in the Red House Museum, together with the excavation notes and photographs.

The Mace excavation, 1957. Collection now housed at The British Museum.

The Campbell excavation, 1968–9. The material is retained by the excavator at the University of Oxford pending the preparation of the report.

The Peacock excavation, 1970. The material is retained by the excavator at the University of Southampton pending the preparation of the report.

Chance finds. Chance finds for the most part found their way into the Red House Museum. The principal objects held include:

 (1) enamelled bracelet found on the north shore in 1952;
 (2) collared urn found near barrow 4 in 1958;
 (3) Bronze Age vessels from the vicinity of barrow 1 found in 1935;
 (4) bronze axe from near barrow 10, found in 1953.

Appendix B
The Hengistbury barrows

In the following paragraphs brief descriptions are offered of the barrows comprising the Hengistbury Bronze Age cemetery. The barrows excavated by Bushe-Fox were described by him in his published Research Report (Bushe-Fox 1915, 14–20). Those examined by St George Gray were never published, but his manuscript excavation notes, upon which the present descriptions are based, are preserved in the Red House Museum, Christchurch. The barrow finds from the Bushe-Fox excavations are in the collection of Sir George Meyrick; those which survive from St George Gray's work are in the Red House Museum.

For the locations of the barrows see fig. 3 (p. 15).

Barrow 1. A low mound 40 m in diameter, 1 m high, apparently undisturbed. Two small vessels of Bronze Age date were found near by in 1935 (fig. 7, nos. 5 and 6).

Barrow 2. A low mound, possibly a barrow. Unexcavated and now obscured by bracken.

Barrow 3 (Bushe-Fox, barrow 1). A large mound composed of gravel and sand measuring some 30 m in diameter and 2 m high. It appears that the barrow had been dug into in the eighteenth century, at which time an urn and some bones were found (Grose 1779). Bushe-Fox found another burial which the earlier excavators had missed, presumably because it lay off-centre. The deposit consisted of an inverted collared urn (fig. 7, no. 1), which contained the cremated remains of an individual about twenty years old, an incense cup (fig. 7, no. 4), two gold cones which would once have covered buttons of an organic material, a halberd pendant of amber and copper alloy and three small amber beads (fig. 6).

Barrow 4 (St George Gray, mound B). An oval mound, probably a mutilated round barrow. It was extensively excavated by St George Gray in 1919, but no trace of a burial was discovered. In 1958, however, part of a collared urn (fig. 7, no. 7) was found in a telephone cable trench dug along the fringe of the mound (Calkin 1964, 9). In all probability this vessel represents a secondary burial, unless it was a fragment of the primary burial which had been discarded by earlier barrow diggers, or even displaced by the rabbits which St George Gray records had infested the mound.

Barrow 5 (St George Gray, mound A). A small barrow *c.* 18 m in diameter. The mound was excavated by St George Gray in 1919, but no burials were discovered.

Barrow 6 (Bushe-Fox, barrow III). A mound of gravel and sand 12·8 m in diameter and 1·2 m high. Nothing appears to have been found in the centre, possibly because of earlier robbing, but towards the periphery five separate deposits were encountered: four were represented by groups of potsherds, two of these being mixed with black charcoaly soil, the fifth consisted of an extensive patch of burnt oak without pottery. It seems probable that we are dealing with a number of secondary burials which had been extensively disturbed, probably by rabbits. The potsherds which can be reconstructed represent two collared urns, of which one now survives (fig. 7, no. 2).

Barrow 7 (Bushe-Fox, barrow II). A mound composed largely of sand, measuring 30 m in diameter and 2 m in height. No central burial was found but a number of, presumably, secondary burials were recorded. One consisted of a cremation contained in a biconical urn of Cornish type, two others were cremations associated with collared urns. In addition two simple examples of southern food vessels were discovered, apparently without cremations (fig. 8). Bushe-Fox records two other vessels which disintegrated and eight separate pockets containing 'burnt matter'.

Barrow 8 (St George Gray, mound C). An apparent barrow examined by St George Gray in 1922. Gray found nothing and concluded that the mound was a natural formation.

Barrow 9 (St George Gray, mound E). A mound now 12 m in diameter but originally considerably larger. The barrow was examined by Gray in 1919, who records the discovery of a number of fragments of a pot of Bronze Age type, decorated with cord impressions 'inside and outside of the angular rim'. The vessel cannot now be traced.

Barrow 10 (St George Gray, mound F). Barrow some 14 m in diameter excavated by St George Gray in 1919. The barrow had been extensively disturbed in previous excavations and no burial remains were found. However, near by, in 1953, a few metres to the west of the barrow, a bronze axe was found 60 cm below the surface (fig. 9, no. 3). Though corroded, it is clearly of Early Bronze Age type and may well once have accompanied a burial either in a flat grave or beneath a barrow which has since been removed.

Barrow 11 (St George Gray, mound G). Barrow, 12m in diameter. The mound was excavated by St George Gray in 1919, who considered that it had already been extensively disturbed by previous excavation. No burial remains were noted.

Barrow 12 (St George Gray, mound H). A mound 10 m in diameter and 0·7 m high, which was extensively excavated by St George Gray in 1919. He records the discovery of three vessels, a collared urn standing upright on its base, a small urn of 'unctious clay' of which only the base remained, and part of another vessel with an 'encircling ridge' which proved to be very fragile. Of these only the collared urn is extant (fig. 7, no. 3). All three seem to have been associated with patches of wood ash.

Barrow 13 (St George Gray, mound J). A mound 14 m in diameter and 0·5 m high, which was excavated by St George Gray in 1919. Gray records the discovery of a complete urn which had been inverted over a cremation. In all some 3 lb of bone were recovered, which were examined by Sir Arthur Keith who identified them as the remains of a woman more than forty years old. Fragments of at least five other pots, apparently without diagnostic characteristics, were noted. The finds cannot now be traced. In addition to the burials three 'burnt areas' were recorded within the mound.

Appendix C
Iron Age coins from Hengistbury

Compiling a complete list of coins from Hengistbury and discovering their present whereabouts has proved to be a task of surprising complexity, and what is offered here can, at best, be regarded only as an interim statement. In preparing these notes I have received much help from the directors and curators of the museums mentioned, and in particular from Miss Melinda Mays, whose detailed study of Durotrigan coinage is now in progress.

The following collections of Hengistbury coins are known:

Durden Collection, late nineteenth century. One Durotrigan A coin, now in the Ashmolean Museum.

Druitt Collection, 1911–c. 1922. The Red House Museum, Christchurch, houses a collection of 18 coins which are recorded in Druitt's handwriting to have been found on Hengistbury between 1911 and 1922. To these may be added a further five coins, labelled by Calkin, which appear to have been found between 1911 and 1916, and probably belong to the Druitt collection. Neither group were included in Allen's list (1961).

Bushe-Fox's excavations, 1911–12. In all, some 3,000 coins were discovered during the excavations. These were briefly discussed and listed by Hill in the excavation report (Bushe-Fox 1915, 63–71) and were again listed according to modern terminology by Allen in his composite list of British coins published in 1961. Some discrepancies occur and it is clear from Allen's comments that several significant coins were neither recognized nor noted in the original publication.

Following the initial identifications, the collection was dispersed. Sir George Meyrick retained 67 Iron Age coins which were carefully listed by Hill (Letter: Hill to Meyrick, 6.iv.1914). 44, including '3 gold, 11 silver, 28 copper and 2 potin', were donated to the British Museum (Letter: Kenyon to Meyrick, 1.x.1913). On Hill's advice (Letter to Meyrick, 24.vi.1913), it would seem that the remainder were split up and given in batches to provincial museums. Records exist of 25 coins being given to the Ashmolean (receipt to Meyrick undated) and 21 to the Fitzwilliam (receipt to Meyrick, 12.viii.1913). The Dorset County Museum received 33 examples from Meyrick in 1916, 19 were presented to Druitt in 1913, 9 to the Winchester City Museum in 1922, and 19 (including 2 of the Coriosolites) were deposited in the Russell Cotes Museum, Bournemouth (now on loan to the Red House Museum). The fate of the remainder is difficult to trace since the relevant records in the British

Museum were destroyed during the war. Evans seems to have acquired 13 examples and the Allen Collection included 4. Both collections, possibly but not certainly, deriving from the original Bushe-Fox find, are now in the Ashmolean Museum.

Much confusion exists. For example, according to Allen's list, the British Museum appears to have 65 coins from the 1911–12 excavation, 21 in excess of the number for which the receipt was given, and more recently, in 1957, Bristol City Museum acquired 10 coins which may have originated from the original excavation, though their ancestry is obscure. Clearly it will be a difficult, if not impossible, task to reconstruct the original collection.

St George Gray's excavations, 1918–24. St George Gray's manuscript notes record the discovery of 2 coins of the 'Channel Islands type' and 17 others which may have been pre-Roman. The St George Gray collection in the Red House Museum now includes 2 coins of the Coriosolites, 3 Durotrigan A and 2 Durotrigan C. Winchester City Museum purchased 7 coins (3 Durotrigan C and 4 Durotrigan D) from Calkin in 1948, which are said to have come from the St George Gray excavations.

The Red House Museum—miscellaneous collections of uncertain origin. In addition to having the Druitt Collection, the St George Gray Collection, the isolated find of 1957 (see below) and the group of coins (probably from the 1911–12 excavations) on loan from the Russell Cotes Museum, the Red House Museum, Christchurch, retains a miscellaneous collection of 45 Durotrigan coins marked 'Hengistbury' or 'Hengistbury type' for which no other details survive. This amorphous collection presumably includes the 19 coins from the 1911–12 excavation which were given to Druitt by Sir George Meyrick, as well as isolated finds collected by Druitt and by the Museum in the period from 1910 to the present day.

Peacock's excavation, 1970. Seven potin coins of Allen's class I were discovered. They are retained by the excavator pending publication.

Isolated finds, 1957. Allen (1961) records the discovery of a Durotrigan B quarter stater in 1957. The coin was presented to the Red House Museum by Marchese Nobili Vitelleschi. He also notes the discovery of a quarter stater of the Coriosolites found in the same year, now in the British Museum.

Isolated find, 1976. A gold 'bullet' of Gallo-Belgic XB type was discovered in 1976. Purchased by the Russell Cotes Museum, Bournemouth.

Bournemouth Art Gallery and Museum. The museum holds a collection of 100 coins (6 Durotrigan A, 73 Durotrigan C, 16 Durotrigan D and 5 examples of uncertain type) which were collected early this century, most of them between 1911 and 1914 at the time when the Head was ploughed. Apart from five Durotrigan C which come from the Bushe-Fox excavations and were donated by Sir George Meyrick, the rest appear to have been donated (or sold) to the museum by several local collectors.

List of coins from Hengistbury

Gallo-Belgic DC	1 AV $\frac{1}{4}$ stater	Bushe-Fox	BM
Gallo-Belgic XB	1 AV	1976 chance find	RCM
British A	1 AV	Druitt collection	BM
British B	1 AV	Bushe-Fox	M
British Lb	1 AV	Bushe-Fox	M
British O	3 AV $\frac{1}{4}$ staters	Bushe-Fox	BM, M

Dobunni

Uninscribed C-I	9 + AR	Bushe-Fox	BM(4)
	2 AR	Druitt collection	RHM
Uninscribed N	1 AR	Bushe-Fox	BM?
ANTED-RIG	1 + AR	Bushe-Fox	BM
EISV	3 + AR	Bushe-Fox	BM(2) M(1)

Durotriges

A	some AR	Bushe-Fox	BM(8)
	9 AR	Druitt collection	RHM
	1 AR	Durden collection	AM
	3 AR	St George Gray	RHM
	6 AR	1911–14	BCM
B	*c.* 19 AR $\frac{1}{4}$ staters	Bushe-Fox	BM
	2 AR $\frac{1}{4}$ staters	Druitt collection	RHM
	4 AR $\frac{1}{4}$ staters	Uncertain	RHM
	1 AR $\frac{1}{4}$ stater	1957 chance find	RHM
C	*c.* 1308 AE	Bushe-Fox	various (see p. 44)
	7 AE	Druitt collection	RHM
	19 AE	Uncertain	RHM
	5 AE	St George Gray	RHM(2), WCM(3)
	6 AE	Uncertain	BCM
	68 AE	1911–14	BCM
D	*c.* 1660 AE	Bushe-Fox	various (see p. 44)
	18 AE	Uncertain	RHM
	1 AE	Druitt collection	RHM
	4 AE	St George Gray	WCM
	4 AE	Uncertain	BCM
	16 AE	1911–14	BCM
E	6 AR $\frac{1}{4}$ staters	Bushe-Fox	BM(4) M(2)

Potin	7 (class 1)	Peacock	(with excavator)
Amorican			
Namnetes	1 AV	Bushe-Fox	M
	1 AV $\frac{1}{4}$ stater	Druitt collection	BM
Coriosolites	11 + AR	Bushe-Fox	BM(2), RHM(2), M(3)
	1 AR $\frac{1}{4}$ stater	Bushe-Fox	BM
	1 AR $\frac{1}{4}$ stater	1957 chance find	BM
	2 AR	St George Gray	RHM
Abrincatui	1 AR	Bushe-Fox	RCM
	1 AR $\frac{1}{4}$ stater	Bushe-Fox	BM
Baiocasses	1 AR $\frac{1}{4}$ stater	Bushe-Fox	BM
Osismii	? 1 AR $\frac{1}{4}$ stater	Bushe-Fox	?
British/Gaulish D	2 AR	Bushe-Fox	M
British/Gaulish E	1 AR	Bushe-Fox	M
British/Gaulish F	1 AR	Bushe-Fox	M

Note: the following abbreviations have been used:

AM: Ashmolean Museum
BCM: Bristol City Museum
BM: British Museum
M: Collection of Sir George Meyrick
RCM: Russell Cotes Museum, Bournemouth
RHM: Red House Museum, Christchurch
WCM: Winchester City Museum

Bibliography

Allen, D. F. 1961. The origins of coinage in Britain: a reappraisal, in Frere, S. S. (ed.), *Problems of the Iron Age in Southern Britain* (London), 97–308.

Allen, D. F. 1968. The Celtic coins, in Richmond 1968, 43–57.

Annable, F. K., and Simpson, D. D. A. 1964. *Guide Catalogue of the Neolithic and Bronze Age Collections in Devizes Museum* (Devizes).

ApSimon, A. M., and Greenfield, E. 1972. The excavation of the Bronze Age and Iron Age settlement at Trevisker Round, St Eval, Cornwall, *Proc. Prehist. Soc.* xxxviii, 302–81.

Bertin, D. 1975. Préliminaire une étude de l'âge du fer en Normandie: inventaire et répartition des sites du Hallstatt et de la Tène, *Annales de Normandie* xxv, 227–40.

Brailsford, J. W. 1958. Early Iron Age 'C' in Wessex, *Proc. Prehist. Soc.* xxiv, 101–19.

Brailsford, J. W. 1962. *Hod Hill* I (London).

Briard, J. 1965. *Les Depôts Bretons et l'Age du Bronze Atlantique* (Rennes).

Briard, J., and Giot, P.-R. 1963. Fouille d'un tumulus de l'Age du Bronze à Saint-Jude en Bourbriac (Côtes-du-Nord), *Annales de Bretagne* lxx, 5–24.

Bushe-Fox, J. P. 1915. *Excavations at Hengistbury Head, Hampshire, in 1911–12* (Oxford).

Caillaud, R., and Lagnel, E. 1946. Une station de la Tène finale à Villers-sur-Mers (Calvados), *Annales de Normandie* xiv, 83–102.

Calkin, J. B. 1954. Bronze implements, hoards of coins, etc., from around Bournemouth, *Proc. Bourn. Nat. Sc. Soc.* xliii, 57–67.

Calkin, J. B. 1962. The Bournemouth area in the Middle and Late Bronze Age with the 'Deverel-Rimbury' problem reconsidered, *Arch. Journ.* cxix, 1–65.

Calkin, J. B. 1966. *Discovering Prehistoric Bournemouth and Christchurch* (Christchurch).

Calkin, J. B. 1969. The population of Neolithic and Bronze Age Dorset and the Bournemouth area, *Proc. Dorset Nat. Hist. & Arch. Soc.* xc, 207–29.

Calkin, J. B., and Green, J. F. N. 1949. Palaeoliths and terraces near Bournemouth, *Proc. Prehist. Soc.* xv, 21–37.

Chapotat, G. 1970. *Vienne Gauloise: Le Matériel de la Tène III trouvé sur la Colline de Sainte-Blandine* (Lyon).

Clarke, R. R. 1954. The Early Iron Age treasure from Snettisham, Norfolk, *Proc. Prehist. Soc.* xx, 27–86.

Colbert de Beaulieu, J.-B. 1956. Notules de numismatique Celtique, *Ogam* viii, 417–30.

Colbert de Beaulieu, J.-B. 1958. Armorican coin hoards in the Channel Islands, *Proc. Prehist. Soc.* xxiv, 201–10.

Colbert de Beaulieu, J.-P. 1973. *Traité de Numismatique Celtique* I (Paris).

Cunliffe, B. 1974. *Iron Age Communities in Britain* (London).

Cunliffe, B. 1976. The origins of urbanization in Britain, in Cunliffe, B., and Rowley, T. (eds.), *Oppida: the Beginnings of Urbanization in Barbarian Europe* (Oxford), 135–62.

Cunliffe, B. 1977. Danebury, Hampshire: second interim report on the excavations 1971–5, *Antiq. Journ.* lvi, 198–216.

Giot, P.-R. 1960. *Brittany* (London).

Giot, P.-R., Deunff, J., Briard, J., and L'Helgouach, J. 1958. L'habitat protohistorique du Moulin-de-la-Rive en Locquirec (Finistère), *Annales de Bretagne* lxv, 27–32.

Giot, P.-R., and Bourhis, J. 1964. Sur une remarquable céramique Gauloise de l'île Gaignog, *Annales de Bretagne* lxxi, 61–6.

Giot, P.-R., Lecerf, Y., and Onnée, Y. 1971. *Céramique Armoricaine de l'Age du Fer* II (Rennes).

Giot, P.-R., Le Roux, C.-T., and Onnée, Y. 1968. *Céramique Armoricaine de l'Age du Fer* (Rennes).

Green, J. F. N. 1946. The terraces of Bournemouth, Hants, *Proc. Geol. Assoc.* lvii, 82ff.

Grose, F. 1779. A description of an ancient fortification near Christchurch, Hampshire, *Archaeologia* v, 237–40.

Hawkes, J. 1937. *The Archaeology of the Channel Islands* II. *The Bailiwick of Jersey* (Jersey).

Hill, G. F. 1911. A hoard of Roman and British coins, *Num. Chron.*, 1911, 42–56.

Kendrick, T. D. 1928. *The Archaeology of the Channel Islands* I. *The Bailiwick of Guernsey* (London).

Le Bihan, J. P., and Galliou, P. 1974. Les forges antiques de Quimper–Kermoisan, *Archéologie en Bretagne* iv, 7–20.

Le Roux, C.-T. 1967. Le souterrain de L'Age du Fer de Stang-Vihan, en Concarneau (Finistère), *Annales de Bretagne* lxxiv, 127–46.

Le Roux, C.-T., and Lecerf, Y. 1973. La céramique du souterrain de l'Age du Fer de Kermoysan en Plabennec (Finistère), *Annales de Bretagne* lxxx, 89–104.

Longworth, I. H. 1961. The origins and development of the primary series in the collared urn tradition in England and Wales, *Proc. Prehist. Soc.* xxvii, 263–306.

Mace, A. 1959. The excavation of a Late Upper Palaeolithic open-site on Hengistbury Head, Christchurch, Hants, *Proc. Prehist. Soc.* xxv, 233–59.

Maxwell, I. S. 1972. The location of Ictis, *Journ. Royal Inst. of Cornwall*, vi, 293–319.

Nash, D. 1976. The growth of urban society in France, in Cunliffe, B., and Rowley, R. T. (eds.), *Oppida: the Beginnings of Urbanization in Barbarian Europe* (Oxford), 95–134.

Peacock, D. P. S. 1969. A contribution to the study of Glastonbury ware from southwestern Britain, *Antiq. Journ.* xlix, 41–61.

Peacock, D. P. S. 1971. Roman amphorae in pre-Roman Britain, in Jesson, M., and Hill, D. (eds.), *The Iron Age and its Hillforts* (Southampton), 161–88.

Piggott, S. 1938. The Early Bronze Age in Wessex, *Proc. Prehist. Soc.* iv, 52–106.

Richmond, I. A. 1968. *Hod Hill* II (London).

Rodwell, W. 1976. Coinage, oppida and the rise of Belgic power in south-eastern Britain, in Cunliffe, B., and Rowley, R. T. (eds.), *Oppida: the Beginnings of Urbanization in Barbarian Europe* (Oxford), 187–367.

Sanquer, R. 1975. Circonscription de Bretagne, *Gallia* xxiii, 333–67.

Threipland, L. M. 1945. Excavations in Brittany, Spring 1939, *Arch. Journ.* c, 128–49.

Threipland, L. M. 1956. An Excavation at St Mawgan-in-Pyder, North Cornwall, *Arch. Journ.* cxiii, 33–81.

Ward Perkins, J. B. 1939. Iron Age metal horses' bits of the British Isles, *Proc. Prehist. Soc.* v, 173–92.

Wheeler, R. E. M. 1943. *Maiden Castle, Dorset* (Oxford).

Wheeler, R. E. M., and Richardson, K. M. 1957. *Hillforts of Northern France* (Oxford).

Index